1972

when
PROGRESSIVE ROCK
ruled the world

Kevan Furbank

SONICBOND

sonicbondpublishing.com

Sonicbond Publishing Limited
www.sonicbondpublishing.co.uk
Email: info@sonicbondpublishing.co.uk

First Published in the United Kingdom 2023
First Published in the United States 2023

British Library Cataloguing in Publication Data:
A Catalogue record for this book is available from the British Library

Copyright Kevan Furbank 2023

ISBN 978-1-78952-288-4

Typeset in ITC Garamond & ITC Avant Garde
Printed and bound in England

Graphic design and typesetting: Full Moon Media

1972
when
PROGRESSIVE ROCK
ruled the world

Contents

Would you like to write for Sonicbond Publishing?

At Sonicbond Publishing we are always on the look-out for authors, particularly for our two main series:

On Track. Mixing fact with in depth analysis, the On Track series examines the work of a particular musical artist or group. All genres are considered from easy listening and jazz to 60s soul to 90s pop, via rock and metal.

On Screen. This series looks at the world of film and television. Subjects considered include directors, actors and writers, as well as entire television and film series. As with the On Track series, we balance fact with analysis.

While professional writing experience would, of course, be an advantage the most important qualification is to have real enthusiasm and knowledge of your subject. First-time authors are welcomed, but the ability to write well in English is essential.

Sonicbond Publishing has distribution throughout Europe and North America, and all books are also published in E-book form. Authors will be paid a royalty based on sales of their book.

Further details are available from www.sonicbondpublishing.co.uk. To contact us, complete the contact form there or email info@sonicbondpublishing.co.uk

Introduction

It was the year of Watergate in the US, the miners' strike in the UK, murder at the Munich Olympics, Bloody Friday bombings in Belfast and cannibalism among jet crash survivors in the Andes. It was also the year a much maligned but much-loved (and, as it turns out, surprisingly resilient) genre of popular music arguably reached its zenith.

In 1972, bands such as Yes, Jethro Tull, Genesis, Gentle Giant, The Strawbs and Can produced albums that, more than 50 years later, are still regarded by many as the pinnacles of their achievements, their Mona Lisas, their Notre Dames, viewed with a mixture of adoration and awe. Some of these bands never produced anything quite as good ever again, even though they tried and, for a few, are still trying.

Many of them managed in that year to achieve the difficult balance between artistic fulfilment and critical acclaim. When the naysayers cast their slings and arrows at prog, they usually point to the musical endeavours that came later; the Passion Plays, Topographic Oceans and Arthurian dramas on ice that became bywords for ludicrous pomposity and bloated excess.

But in 1972, the genre was still fresh, new and exciting. Not only that, it was popular! Albums from Jethro Tull, Pink Floyd, Emerson, Lake & Palmer, Yes, Santana and The Moody Blues all reached the Top Ten in the UK charts – in the US, the Tull album had two weeks at number one. Today, it's a cause for celebration when a prog album manages to limp its way into the lower reaches of the Top 40. In 1972, you could walk along the street with a copy of *Close to the Edge* under your arm and you wouldn't be subjected to derision and abuse. Truly, the past is a different country.

For this book, I have chosen 22 progressive rock albums that I consider to be classics of the genre – influential, inspiring and downright entertaining. We can argue all night about whether these are the best albums the bands produced – that is, of course, a wholly subjective opinion. In any case, our favourite albums tend to be the first ones we heard, that served as gateways into the music. But these are albums that achieved critical acclaim and, sometimes, commercial success. And they have stood the test of time; 50 years later, we are still talking about them and listening to them, and they are still inspiring modern progressive rock bands.

With a shortlist of 22, it's likely that one of your own personal favourites hasn't got a look-in. That's why I include a section on albums that deserve a mention in despatches, the ones that also served to make the year a little more colourful than it might otherwise have been. I also look at where progressive rock went next, and why it has seen a remarkable resurgence in the last few decades.

You will note that half of the albums I have chosen are British. This is not because I'm a rabid, xenophobic Englishman. It's because, in the beginning, progressive rock was a particularly British phenomenon, perhaps because of our innate pomposity and pretensions. You will rarely, in my experience, find a race with their heads stuck so firmly up their own backsides, although we're always ready to joke about it. But within my list, you will also find bands from the US, Germany, Holland, Italy, Greece and Sweden. Oh, and there will also be some yodelling.

So join me in my musical time machine as we journey some 50 years into the past, to a time when prog ruled the world. Well, almost...

The Solid Time of Change

Ask Alexa, or any other of your chosen personal digital assistants, to play music from 1972, and you will be lucky to hear any prog. But you will be reminded (or, if you are too young to remember, you will discover) that the musical landscape was wide and varied, certainly compared to the homogenised output of the 2020s. Indeed, I may go so far as to say 'eclectic', defined as deriving ideas, style, or taste from a broad and diverse range of sources.

It was the year of the singer/songwriter, such as Carole King, Cat Stevens and James Taylor; the beginning of glam rock, with hits from David Bowie, Elton John and T-Rex; when Motown joined the black power movement and Michael Jackson began forging his solo career. There were pretty boy singers such as David Cassidy and Donny Osmond, classic hits by easy-listening siblings, The Carpenters, and cries of defiance from 50s and 60s throwbacks including Elvis Presley, Chuck Berry and The Rolling Stones.

Even The Beatles were still at it, albeit as individuals instead of a Fab Four – John Lennon released the politically-charged and critically-panned album *Some Time in New York City* and commercially-toxic single 'Woman is the N****r of the World'; Paul McCartney reached the UK Top 20 with the equally-controversial 'Give Ireland Back to the Irish', the risible 'Mary Had a Little Lamb' and the banned 'Hi Hi Hi'; Ringo Starr had a hit with 'Back Off Boogaloo'; and George Harrison pre-empted Live Aid by releasing a live recording of his Bangla Desh fundraising concert.

Swirling about in this musical soup were the chunky bits of progressive rock. Like all musical genres, it didn't suddenly appear fully formed from out of the ether like Captain James T. Kirk arriving unannounced on a primitive planet. It evolved from earlier forms of music, such as psychedelic rock – indeed, it is sometimes difficult to see where one ends and the other begins. In 1967, Pink Floyd were the quintessential psychedelic rock band, producing three-minute nursery rhyme-style streams of consciousnesses or rambling, 20-minute sound collages with light-show accompaniment. By 1972, they were a prog band on the cusp of releasing the biggest prog album of all time.

Readers of my previous book, *The Psychedelic Rock of 1967* (still available at all good online booksellers; don't all rush at once) will know that I frequently blame/credit The Beatles for most of the musical changes since 1963 – and I'm going to do so again. But that's not just my view; here's Yes and King Crimson drummer Bill Bruford making the exact same point to *Modern Drummer* magazine in 2007:

Without The Beatles, or someone else who had done what The Beatles did, it is fair to assume that there would have been no progressive rock... They broke down every barrier that ever existed. Suddenly you could do anything after The Beatles. You could write your own music, make it 90 yards long, put it in 7/4, whatever you wanted.

What The Beatles did, first and foremost, was to give artistic control to the artists. Previously, all decisions were taken by blokes in suits smoking fat cigars; managers, A&R men, record company bosses and producers called the shots and decided on the songs the artists would perform and how to record them. Then four cheeky Scousers came along who had their own ideas, and gradually took control of the content, sound and presentation of their own material.

It helped that they were on a minor EMI label, Parlophone, and were being produced by one of the younger employees at the EMI studios in Abbey Road who had cut his teeth on comedy records. And it also helped that The Beatles were talented songwriters who churned out hit after hit and made everyone concerned oodles of money. When they gave up touring in 1966, they spent most of their time in the studio tinkering, experimenting, innovating and spending months on end coming up with their next masterpiece.

By 1967, record companies were giving other bands free rein in the studio and trusting they would come up with the goods. And most of the time, they did because they were the same age and on the same wavelength as the fans buying the records. So by 1972, the artist was king and the studio was his or her domain – the idea that a manager or record company executive would have a say in the creation of the actual music had become a heresy in certain quarters. If a band wanted to take a year to create its masterpiece, then that's what happened. The role of the record company was to be patient and wait for the magic to happen, while the role of the manager was to dangle concert promoters off the edge of balconies to make sure the artists got paid.

Technological changes also played a part. In 1967, The Beatles made *Sgt Pepper's Lonely Hearts Club Band* with four-track recording machines. If you had more than four instruments and voices to record, you had to mix as you went along, then 'bounce' what you had to one track and wipe the other three clean to record the harmonies, or a sitar, or 20 pianos playing one chord in unison. The Fab Four didn't have eight-track until *Abbey Road* in 1969.

By 1972, most studios had sixteen-track recorders, which gave artists much more freedom to do what they wanted and, consequently, enabled them to tinker for much, much longer. But, remember, this was still in the days before digital recording when editing meant literally taking a razor blade to a piece of tape. The days of being able to cut and paste at a touch of a mouse were still a long way off.

Other innovations were the development of the compact cassette and a machine that could record on them. The Beatles had to write memorable songs because that was the only way they could remember them. But by the late 1960s, artists could capture all their brilliant musical thoughts at home to present to the rest of the band in the studio, so the best bits could be cherry-picked and combined into something new and exciting. In 1972, Teac introduced four-track tape recorders for home use, so musicians could create entire songs in their living rooms.

They also had more instruments to play with. The mighty Mellotron, introduced in 1963, was heard in 1967 on The Beatles' 'Strawberry Fields Forever' and on The Moody Blues' album *Days of Future Passed*. But it was a big, unwieldy and unpredictable monster of a machine that practically required a degree in engineering to operate and a forklift truck to manoeuvre. In 1970, that changed with the introduction of the smaller, more lightweight Model 400 – now the Mellotron could actually be taken on tour and used on stage, so it became the must-have instrument for a lot of progressive rock bands who wanted that big orchestral sound, particularly King Crimson and Genesis.

Portable synthesisers became more widespread and, indeed, more portable. In 1970, Robert Moog introduced the Minimoog, which was about the size of a typewriter, while a year later, Malcolm Cecil and Margouleff debuted The Original New Timbral Orchestra, or TONTO, which could produce different synthesised sounds simultaneously.

In my 1967 book, I showed how changes in society, such as the improvement in education, the growing affluence of teenagers and the widening gap between generations, created a growing market for psychedelic rock. As these trends continued into the 1970s, they allowed progressive rock to briefly take centre stage.

For example, record buyers could more easily afford long-players, so the importance of singles began to diminish, and the LP became the ultimate artistic statement. In the UK, it was a long-standing tradition not to put the hit single on the album as it was feared fans would baulk at paying for the same song twice (in the US, the opposite approach was taken – the album wouldn't sell unless it contained the hit). But by 1972, some bands had dispensed with singles completely – unless the record companies sneaked them out without their knowledge – seeing the constraints and triviality of the three-minute pop platter as being beneath them.

With up to 26 minutes of music space available on each side of an LP, artists began to stretch beyond the traditional song length of two to four minutes. Now, long songs were nothing brand, spanking new – classical music was always as long as the composers wanted it to be, simply because recording technology constraints didn't exist. The compact disc was initially designed to hold 74 minutes of music so the listener could hear Beethoven's Ninth Symphony without interruption.

Jazz artists frequently created lengthy suites of music – John Coltrane's *A Love Supreme*, released in 1964, originally contained an eighteen-minute track stretching across side two. In folk music, Arlo Guthrie and Sandy Bull experimented with side-long songs, while you could argue that *Days of Future Passed* contains two side-long pieces of music, with each song connected by orchestral links.

But it was in 1972 that the epic long song became ubiquitous, with 'Supper's Ready' by Genesis, 'Close to the Edge' by Yes, Jethro Tull's 'Thick as a Brick' and 'Anonymous' by Focus all testing the listener's patience and bladder control. Some of these compositions began life as separate pieces until someone said, 'Hey, we can link these together', while others were always intended to be monsters – Ian Anderson of Jethro Tull deliberately set out to create a spoof concept album that would contain one piece of shifting, changing music, separated only by some windy sound effects that told you it was time to turn the record over.

The other social change that helped the development of progressive rock was education. Most songs are about love, and there's nothing wrong with that. It makes the world go round and is allegedly all you need. Even the term 'rock 'n' roll' was a euphemism for the, ahem, physical demonstration of mutual attraction. When the bands of the 1950s were rockin', rollin' and shakin' all over, they were, of course, singing about shagging.

But by the 1960s, young musicians had a wider palette of knowledge to draw from. Instead of being simple country boys or high school dropouts, they were graduating from art schools and universities with their heads full of literature and philosophy. It was inevitable that these ideas would find their way into the music. Elvis Presley sang, 'Well, there's-a one for the money'. John Lennon sang 'Turn off your mind, relax and float downstream', quoting *The Tibetan Book of the Dead*. Jon Anderson of Yes made a career out of crafting dense, impenetrable lyrics inspired by such popular bestsellers as *Autobiography of a Yogi* by Paramahansa Yogan. Sure, we've all got a dog-eared copy in the bookcase.

With their heads full of stories, legends, myths and philosophies, prog artists wanted to do more than just write three-minute love songs – they wanted to spread ideas and tell tales through music and lyrics. Thus the concept album became ubiquitous. Again, the idea of creating a collection of songs that tell a story or are linked thematically was not a new, er, concept – Woody Guthrie did it with his 1940 album *Dust Bowl Ballads*, Frank Sinatra with his themed series of LPs for Capitol Records in the 1950s, and jazz artists such as Duke Ellington, whose 1957 release *Such Sweet Thunder* is a suite of melodies inspired by the works of William Shakespeare.

But it took the proggers to make the concept album a ubiquitous part of the musical landscape, and by 1972, it was rare to find a prog album that didn't have some sort of theme running through the grooves and seeping into the cover artwork. The ultimate concept album was probably *Thick as a Brick*, on which more time was spent creating the lavish packaging than on recording the music.

Prog artists were also more musically educated. Keith Emerson and Rick Wakeman, for example, had piano lessons from an early age and learnt how to read music. Wakeman also played clarinet. As for the three Shulman brothers, who formed the core of Gentle Giant, they were encouraged by their jazz trumpeter father to master as many instruments as they could. Another Giant, Kerry Minnear, graduated from the Royal Academy of

Music in London and played eleven instruments on the band's first album, including cello.

So musical proficiency became one of the bedrocks of progressive rock, to a point where even the drummer brought an academic approach to his (and it was usually a he) instruments, augmenting the basic setup of toms, bass drum and cymbals with all manner of things to hit, stroke and shake. Gone were the days when the drummer or bass player would wait for the guitarist and singer to decide how the song should go. Instead, every member of the band could throw in ideas, helping to stretch compositions even further or make a case for a short musical interlude involving double or triple-tracked bass guitar, or an acoustic guitar solo, or a burst of manic percussion in a time signature previously only known to Stephen Hawking.

With musical proficiency came a wider palette of influences. Keith Emerson of The Nice and ELP was inspired by Fats Waller, Oscar Peterson, Bach, Copland and Bartok. Rick Wakeman of The Strawbs and Yes loved (and probably still does) Trad Jazz, Prokofiev and Lonnie Donegan. Steve Howe of Yes credits Tennessee Ernie Ford, Barney Kessel and Chet Atkins. For Steve Hackett of Genesis, it was The Shadows and Segovia. For Evángelos Odysséas Papathanassíou – aka Vangelis, of Aphrodite's Child – it was the Greek folk music of his youth. Frank Zappa's musical career was kickstarted by the sound experiments of Edgard Varese but he also loved cheesy doo-wop.

All these influences inevitably found their way into the music they were making, by accident and by design, with the result that prog opened its arms and embraced any and all genres, stretching back into the distant past. Listen to Gentle Giant and you will hear baroque influences from the 17th century and even earlier. And you know what they say – if it ain't baroque, don't fix it.

New World

We could argue until the cows come home, make a cup of tea and sit down to listen to an entire box set over what was the first progressive rock album. Some commentators go back to The Beatles' *Revolver* or The Beach Boys' *Pet Sounds*. Others of a more purist bent wait until 1969 with *In the Court of the Crimson King*. But I am going to stick my neck out and give the honour to The Moody Blues' 1967 creation: *Days of Future Passed*.

Why? Well, first of all, it's a concept album – a day in the life, as it were, from dawn to night, with every song serving the story. To understand it properly, you have to listen from beginning to end, from 'The Day Begins' to 'Late Lament' (passing through 'Nights in White Satin', which, in 1972, became a belated hit single for the band). In doing so, it embraces rock, pop, soaring ballads, exotic Eastern scales and portentous poetry.

It's also a classical and rock mash-up – initially intended to be an adaptation of Dvorak's New World Symphony, it instead used an orchestra to link original songs into side-long suites, with conductor Peter Knight reprising melodic themes and composing new material to open and close the album. This isn't just a collection of songs with classical backing – it is the orchestra and rock band weaving in and out to create a whole new musical experience.

And there's a mighty Mellotron! Everywhere! In fact, it's almost impossible to tell where the orchestra ends and the Mellotron begins. They blend together so well.

Psychedelic rock was made under the influence of LSD – that's why it was psychedelic, maaan. But *Days of Future Passed* was so precise and intricate, it could only be made by musicians fuelled by nothing more stimulating than a cup of tea and some biscuits. It is a prog pioneer.

The Moodies continued in a similar vein but never reached the prog heights of their 1967 masterpiece. Never mind, there were plenty of other bands ready and willing to pick up the prog baton and wave it around. The Nice, led by keyboard maestro Emerson, went full-on prog for their second album, 1968's *Ars Longa Vita Brevis*, which not only had a Latin title meaning 'Art is long, life is short' but featured a side-long suite inspired by Bach's Brandenburg Concerto No3.

In the same year, the first mention of progressive rock appeared on a record sleeve on the debut album by Canterbury band Caravan. By the following year, prog was taking flight thanks to bands including The Who (Tommy), Pink Floyd (Ummagumma), Amon Duul II (Phallus Dei), Frank Zappa (Uncle Meat) and debuts from Yes, Van Der Graaf Generator and Renaissance.

King Crimson's first LP that year was not only an instant prog classic that blended orchestral music, jazz and hard rock but showed that prog could be downright nasty and dirty. Even now, '21st Century Schizoid Man' sounds like someone's deranged idea of Armageddon while, live, the band channelled Holst's Planets Suite and free jazz. Its importance is perhaps underlined by the fact that, 53 years later, King Crimson were until recently still touring under band leader Robert Fripp and still making music that sounds timeless.

Out of those early albums came a whole panoply of progressive rock sub-genres: progressive jazz, space rock, krautrock, symphonic prog, Rock in Opposition, the Canterbury sound, art rock, zeuhl, prog metal, neo-prog, to name but a few. Many labels, but the same intention – to break free of old restrictions, to demolish old boundaries, to stimulate both the body and the mind, to excite, entertain and inform. To mangle a phrase from Captain James T. Kirk, to boldly go where no music has gone before...

Jethro Tull – *Thick as a Brick*

Personnel
Ian Anderson: vocals, flute, acoustic guitar, violin, saxophone, trumpet
Martin Barre: electric guitar, lute
John Evan: Hammond organ, piano, harpsichord
Jeffrey Hammond: bass, spoken word
Barriemore Barlow: drums, timpani, percussion
With:
David Palmer: strings arrangements & conducting
Recorded during December 1971 at Morgan Studios, London
Produced by Ian Anderson and Terry Ellis
Engineered by Robin Black
Label: Chrysalis (Europe), Reprise (everywhere else)
Release date: 3 March 1972
Chart placings: UK: 5, US: 1, Australia: 1, Canada: 1, Denmark: 1, Norway: 3,
Netherlands: 3, Germany: 4,
Tracks (subtitles taken from 40th-anniversary edition downloads): 'Thick as a
Brick, Part 1' – i) 'Really Don't Mind/See There a Son Is Born' ii) 'The Poet and
the Painter' iii) 'What Do You Do When the Old Man's Gone?/From the Upper
Class' iv) 'You Curl Your Toes in Fun/Childhood Heroes/Stabs Instrumental',
'Thick as a Brick, Part 2' – i) 'See There a Man Is Born/Clear White Circles' ii)
'Legends and Believe in the Day' iii) 'Tales of Your Life' iv) 'Childhood Heroes
Reprise'
All tracks written by Gerald Bostock (but not really)

The story so far...

Originally, they were the John Evan Band, formed by Blackpool schoolmates
Ian Anderson, Jeffrey Hammond and John Evans (he later lost the 's') in 1964.
They recruited drummer Barrie Barlow and guitarist Chris Riley, playing blue-
eyed soul. Various personnel changes saw Hammond replaced on bass by
Glenn Cornick and Riley by Mick Abrahams. By 1967, they were a four-piece
blues band with Clive Bunker on drums. New name Jethro Tull came from
a booking agent's staff member, who was a history buff (Mr Tull invented
the horse-drawn seed drill in 1700), and first single 'Aeroplane' – originally
recorded by the John Evan Smash – released in 1968 on MGM Records
(and famously credited to 'Jethro Toe'). Signed to Island Records, the band
recorded a blues album heavily influenced by Abrahams, who left soon after
(or was pushed). The title, *This Was,* suggested changes to come. Recruiting
new guitarist Martin Barre, leader Anderson took Jethro Tull in the direction
of progressive blues and folk, releasing the UK number one album *Stand Up*
in 1968 and number three single 'Living in the Past'. Follow-up, *Benefit,* in
1970, fared less well despite the return of John Evan on keyboards but 1971's
Aqualung was a million-seller, cracking the US Top 10. Bunker left in May
1971 and was replaced by Barrie Barlow.

The album

They burned copies of Aqualung in the US. It had songs about religion on it that offended the Bible Belt, so they stoked up the fires of righteousness. That was in the days when an album could do that – Ian Anderson released one about religion in 2022 and no one really took much notice. But back in 1971, it seemed a few lyrics about Christianity in the vinyl grooves of a British band's latest LP could make the baby Jesus cry.

Everyone thought it was a concept album about religion, or homelessness, or ... something. Ian Anderson denied it, but no one believed him. After all, that was surely him on the cover, greasy fingers feeling shabby clothes, lurking furtively like some bedraggled, perverted Fagin. And there did seem to be a sort of common theme running through it, something about the lost and dispossessed, abandoned by society but also by the followers of Yahweh, that was referenced in the mock bible verses on the back of the sleeve.

Anyway, the outcry and misinterpretation – as Anderson saw it – led him to make a momentous decision: the next Jethro Tull LP *would* be a concept album. In fact, it would be the mother of all concept albums, a spoof, a parody that would play on the gullibility of some of the fans and critics. And it wouldn't just be the music – the mischief would extend to the elaborate packaging, even to the song credits. What fun! And, in the process, Anderson created one of the greatest progressive rock albums of the 1970s.

In my introduction, I pointed out that many of the progressive rock bands we meet in this book came out of the psychedelic era. Well, Tull were an exception. They were a soul band, then a blues band, before Anderson pulled in elements of prog and folk to create a richer musical stew. But his songwriting inspiration wasn't The Beatles, Stevie Winwood or T-Bone Walker but a fellow Blackpool dweller, one Roy Harper, who penned stark, uncompromising blasts at religion, capitalism, drug laws, racism ... well, anything you've got, really. So vitriolic and impassioned could he be that audiences used to walk out during 'I Hate the White Man', his tirade against white rule in South Africa.

Anderson wasn't the only other musician to be inspired by Harper – Led Zeppelin named a blues song 'Hats Off to (Roy) Harper' on their third album, and he sang 'Have a Cigar' on Pink Floyd's *Wish You Were Here*. But the songwriting influence is clear to see in Anderson's work, particularly in his acoustic numbers, and it's not just that they both wrote songs about Blackpool. It was in their choice of targets, in their biting cynicism, and in their occasionally touching, gentle ballads augmented by strings. What made them different was how their characters dictated the songs – Harper was impassioned, unrestrained, angry, romantic and personal; Anderson more detached and controlled, more likely to create a character than write about himself, to stand outside the song and view it with wry cynicism.

Both also play acoustic guitar, Harper with a distinctive fingerpicking style and Anderson with more of a strumming approach while ringing out individual notes with his pick. The latter is best known for playing the flute while unaccountably standing on one leg, but he started off as a guitarist, changing instruments only when Mick Abrahams joined the band. Assuming the leadership of Tull, and taking the music away from blues purity, allowed him to slip in some acoustic numbers to provide a respite from the thundering drums and roaring electric guitar.

So in 1969's *Stand Up*, we get the wistful 'Reasons For Waiting', on *Benefit*, the folkie 'Sossity, You're a Woman', on *Aqualung*, the brief but beautiful 'Wond'ring Aloud' and 'Slipstream'. But *Thick as a Brick* was to be the first album to have the acoustic guitar centre-stage, opening and closing proceedings and driving many of the sections. It was not an unexpected decision. At the end of 1971, after Barrie Barlow had joined on drums, Tull released an EP containing the pretty acoustic-based 'Life is a Long Song' (along with Anderson's Blackpool tribute, 'Up the Pool') that reached the heady heights of number eleven in the UK charts, the last time the band would make an appearance in the UK Top 30 until 1976.

In fact, when he started composing material for the new album, all Anderson had was an acoustic riff in F (but played as a D with a capo on the third fret) and the line 'Really don't mind if you sit this one out...'. He says he didn't originally envisage the album containing one long track split over two sides of vinyl, and that everything grew as it went along in rehearsals. But at some stage, Anderson conceived the idea of writing a poem that would allegedly spring from the mind of a precocious eight-year-old called Gerald Bostock – giving the imaginary youngster the nickname Little Milton, after the 17th-century poet John Milton.

He has since said that Bostock is an exaggerated version of himself as a child. He told *Prog* magazine in 2016:

As a child, I was a bit of a rebel. Most of my peers aspired to go to grammar school, getting eight O Levels and three A Levels, then becoming part of conventional society. That never appealed to me. I was the sort of child who loved spending time collecting pond life and then analysing it. I also loved science fiction stories of the era (the 1950s), because they told of a different, exciting future. So, I stood apart from others of my age and drew on this for the character of Gerald Bostock. But he himself is a fiction.

As to the content of Little Milton's ramblings, well, they are somewhat obscure and contain an almost kaleidoscopic jumble of images and references. As the album was meant as a parody, we shouldn't necessarily expect the words to have much meaning anyway. But there are a few themes that come through, ones Anderson has touched on before and will do so again, such as the fragility of modern values, the ephemeral nature of power and the hypocrisy and helplessness of those who seek to rule over us, the dumbing down of education and the drive towards the average rather than the exceptional. Here's another hint to their origin from a 1976 interview with John Alan Simon in *Downbeat* magazine:

> It wasn't a conception, really, just the act of writing a song, thinking about what I might have been, what I began life as being, what kind of childhood images moved me – dealt with in a very oblique fashion, because I'm not setting out to create a threadbare tale of emotional woe or to even delineate emotional happenings. I'm just creating a background lyrical summation of a lot of things I feel about being a contemporary child in this age and the problems that one has – the problems of being precocious beyond one's age or having interests beyond one's age, and, to some extent, being ruled in a kind of heavy-handed, unexplained fashion by father-figures.

Heavy-handed father figures have appeared before in Anderson's work: On 'Son', from *Benefit*, he depicts a toxic father-son relationship – 'Permission to breathe, sir/Don't talk to me like that, I'm your old man' – and in 'Wind-Up', from *Aqualung,* he rages 'How'd you dare to tell me that I'm my father's son, when that was just an accident of birth'. Clearly, there had been some friction between the generations in the Anderson parental home, although probably no more than existed – and still exist – in a lot of homes, and the son paid the father a small tribute by wearing his bedraggled, tramp-like coat on stage.

Anderson also revealed in *Psychology Today*, no less, that he had been caned at school, a common occurrence in Britain at the time and seen as morale and moral-building. Eventually, at seventeen, he refused to be beaten and was kicked out of school instead. So it's clear there are plenty of biographical elements in Gerald Bostock's poetry, but heavily disguised so Anderson can plausibly say, 'It's not about me – I'm writing about some other bugger'. Perhaps writing it was a cathartic experience for Anderson, letting it all out but staying guarded and secretive at the same time.

There's also an awful lot of silliness for silly's sake on *Thick as a Brick* – this is the era of *Monty Python's Flying Circus*, practitioners of the surreal, ridiculous and occasionally subversive humour introduced by Spike Milligan and the Goons. The words were not meant to be taken too seriously; they were a spoof of the apparently dense, murky and faux-intellectual lyrics some bands with an inflated opinion of themselves were producing at the time. Yes, we all know who I'm talking about. So, Anderson created images and ideas that were deliberately ridiculous – the babies wearing nylons, the cats getting an upgrade, the references to Superman and Biggles (fictional pilot and adventurer from 1930s, non-British readers) and the generally jumbled nature of the narrative, which goes nowhere and everywhere at the same time. Taken as poetry, you could rip this to pieces as bloated and unfocused. But as lyrics, they served their purpose – to give Anderson a framework upon which to hang his music.

The band had just finished up a US tour and had December 1971 off to concentrate on creating the next LP. During that time, Anderson would get up early in the morning to write and, in the afternoon, go into The Rolling Stones' basement studio in London with the band to rehearse what he had just composed. The next day, he would write the next section and tack that onto the previous one, so after ten days, they had one long piece made up of about eight distinct parts (the titles listed above were not on the original album but appeared as separate downloadable tracks for the digital version of the 40th-anniversary box set). In the box set, talking to Dom Lawson, he explained:

> It was a very speedy process and, because I was the only writer, it was like being a conductor, trying to get the other guys to realise the masterplan I was evolving. They didn't have the foggiest clue what was going on and they probably thought I was faintly barking... But very quickly, we had it complete and in a form that allowed us to go in and play a lot of it live in the studio.

That was Morgan Studios in Willesden, north-west London, using studio two because it had a more intimate, dryer sound that suited acoustic instruments. Thanks to the earlier rehearsals, the album took about two weeks to record, in the order that the music appears, with a couple more weeks for overdubs. It was a tricky task, requiring engineer Robin Black to ensure he had enough tracks left at the end of each piece of music to start the instruments for the next. In the box set, Black reveals that during the mixing stage, it was discovered the tuning was wrong at the end of side one – the reason was the tape machine had started running slower at the end of 20-odd minutes of tape, so the entire mixing process had to start again from scratch. Black admitted: 'I was quite depressed at this'.

The result is an album that, on side one at least, represents a slice of the most perfect Tullian prog you could hope to hear. From the gentle, whimsical acoustic guitar opening, through the thunderous, repetitive riffing of 'See, there, a son is born', the stomping 'Poet and the Painter', the jig-like 'From the Upper Class' and sprightly 'Childhood Heroes', the first side grows in stature and drama until stabbing chord triplets transition into some windy sound effects, telling us it's time to turn the album over.

Had 74-minute CDs been around in 1972, there's no doubt Anderson would have dispensed with the windy interlude and gone straight into side two, which takes up where the first side left off. The flip side, however, is less successful – less cohesive, bittier, with frequent reprises, some clumsy avant-garde percussion sequences, with barely audible muttering from Jeffrey Hammond, and a rather lengthy and dull section in the middle. It doesn't really take off again until the stately 'Childhood Heroes Reprise' at the end, finishing with a repeat of the opening solo acoustic guitar figure under the line 'And your wise men don't know how it feels to be thick... as a... brick...' and a final sardonic chuckle. And it seems Anderson agrees with me – after being performed in its entirety in 1972, the album settled down as a long-standing part of the Tull live repertoire but as a truncated, 13-minute suite containing most of side one plus the side two ending.

But *Thick as a Brick* is not just about what's in the grooves because we now come to the album's cover: a fold-out, twelve-page A3 newspaper that famously took longer to produce than the music. By any standards you care to invoke, this was the progressive rock cover par excellence, an investment in time, imagination and money that was not to be repeated until the introduction of the wallet-draining box set.

Under Ian Anderson's leadership, Jethro Tull always had a bit of showmanship about them, a desire to surprise and delight the audience visually as well as musically. Anderson also realised that persuading an audience to sit down and listen to 20 or 40 minutes of continuous new music was a very big ask. So Tull added visual silliness to their performances: opening the show with the entire band wearing shabby raincoats, sweeping the stage; having an on-stage telephone answered by a roadie in scuba gear; surprise weather reports and skits about 'non-rabbits'; various band members wearing striped Victorian bathing costumes.

As the band toured Europe in January 1972, Anderson was thinking about what to do with the album's cover, and many of the on-stage shenanigans ended up in the finished artwork. This allowed all the band members to make a contribution – bass player Jeffrey Hammond remembers recording into a Dictaphone and sending the tapes off to secretaries to type up. He added: 'Most of it was giggling, I think, and laughing at some of the more immature sections of it'.

The idea grew that the cover could comprise a newspaper, with a lead story on Gerald Bostock winning a prize for his poetry but then being disqualified following outrage over the 'seriously unbalanced' and 'extremely unwholesome' content of his verses. Other stories touched on the same issue – there was one about Bostock being accused of impregnating fourteen-year-old Julia Fealey, his 'chum, with whom he writes poems', and another revealing that a 'major beat group' would record the poetry as an album. The newspaper even reviews the release – Julian Stone-Mason BA says: 'Not blatantly commercial then, but a fine disc which, although possessing many faults, should do well'.

Elsewhere, the newspaper combines surreal, Python-esque nonsense with the trivial, parochial news that still fills many local newspapers (those that are still left as the internet cuts a swathe of destruction through the industry). So there are references to 'non-rabbits', whatever they are, the fictitious game of Fennel, TV listings featuring such programmes as Handstand, Rocket Jesus Christ and Pyk Owrno Zes, and cinemas advertising films including Lust of a Small Nun. These jostle alongside the Births, Marriages and Deaths columns, a man arrested for throwing a bottle during a lecture and a police hunt for twelve assorted gnomes and four full-size emperor penguins stolen from a garden of Mr R. Black.

All this puerile and juvenile nonsense was handed over to Roy Eldridge, a Chrysalis Records executive who, as a former newspaper journalist, knew how to design something that would ape the ramshackle, amateur appearance of a local rag from the 1970s. The result is something that takes longer to read than the album does to listen to and probably had most record buyers scratching their heads in confusion, particularly if they weren't British and hadn't been brought up on a diet of Neddy Seagoon and dead parrots. Some people didn't like it and thought it was just silly, such as Tull's manager Terry Ellis. Perhaps ex-Beatle John Lennon didn't like it either – his 1972 album, *Some Time in New York City,* also had a newspaper cover but not remotely as well done.

Tull's cover may have been expensive to produce and not welcomed by all but it has passed into progressive rock history and remains a convincing reason to buy the vinyl version of the album. Later issues replaced it with a single cardboard sleeve, so original copies are worth up to £150 (I foolishly filled in the crossword on mine, slashing its second-hand value).

Critics greeted the album with pretty much the same review as the band gave itself in the newspaper – flawed but could do well. *Melody Maker* said the music needed time to be absorbed, *New Musical Express* called it a 'stand-or-fall epic' and *Rolling Stone* said it was 'sophisticated and ground-breaking'. Robert Christgau of *Village Voice* dismissed it as 'the usual shit'. But posterity's rosy glow puts *Thick as a Brick* in its rightful place as 'a masterpiece in the annals of progressive rock' (*AllMusic*), 'not only a pinnacle achievement for Jethro Tull, but also a concrete example of just how adventurous and free artists used to be' (*Pop Matters*), and 'an Olympian feat of composition and musicianship' (*Record Collector*).

Tull would follow up Thick as a Brick with another album-length opus, *A Passion Play,* that would divide audiences even more and lead to the band's apparent (PR-spun) split. 40 years later, Anderson would tell us what happened to Gerald Bostock with *Thick as a Brick 2*, but it's not a patch on the original. The fact is, he never again matched the glory of *Thick as a Brick*, which, today, still stands as one of the greatest progressive rock albums of all time.

Genesis – *Foxtrot*

Personnel
Tony Banks: organ, Mellotron, piano, electric piano, 12-string, voices
Phil Collins: drums, voices, assorted percussion
Peter Gabriel: lead voice, flute, bass drum, tambourine, oboe
Steve Hackett: electric guitar, 12-string and 6-string solos
Michael Rutherford: bass, bass pedals, 12-string guitar, voices, cello
Recorded August to September 1972 at Island Studios, London
Produced by David Hitchcock and Genesis
Engineered by John Burns
Label: Charisma
Release date: 6 October.
Chart placings: UK: 12, Italy: 1
Tracks: 'Watcher of the Skies', 'Time Table', 'Get 'Em Out By Friday', 'Can-Utility and the Coastliners', 'Horizons', 'Supper's Ready' – i) 'Lover's Leap' II) 'The Guaranteed Eternal Sanctuary Man' iii) 'Ikhnaton and Itsacon and the Band of Merry Men' iv) 'How Dare I Be So Beautiful' v) 'Willow Farm' vi) 'Apocalypse in 9/8 (Co-Starring The Delicious Talents of Gabble Ratchet)' vii) 'As Sure as Eggs is Eggs (Aching Men's Feet)'
All titles composed, arranged and performed by Genesis.

The story so far...

Formed in 1967 by Peter Gabriel, Tony Banks, Anthony 'Ant' Phillips, Mike Rutherford and Chris Stewart, all pupils at Charterhouse public school in Surrey and members of previous bands Anon or Garden Wall. An early demo tape was given to record producer Jonathan King, another Charterhouse alumni, who named them Genesis and signed them to Decca Records. It was, apparently, that easy. Early singles were unsuccessful, and drummer Stewart left, replaced by John Silver (also Charterhouse). The album, *From Genesis To Revelation*, released in 1969, sold fewer than 700 copies at the time. Dumped by Decca, they recorded more demos that were rejected by every record label in sight. So, not so easy after all. Silver left, replaced by John Mayhew. Concentrating on live work, they were eventually signed by Charisma, who released their second album, *Trespass*, in 1970. It flopped in the UK but reached number one in Belgium. Phillips, suffering from stage fright, left the group, and Mayhew was fired. Replacements Steve Hackett, on guitar, and Phil Collins, on drums, joined to record *Nursery Cryme*, released in November 1971.

The album

As I penned this chapter, Genesis were saying goodbye for keeps with three final dates at the cavernous O2 Arena in London. Back in 1972, no one would have even dared to suggest that this strange little band formed by posh Englishmen from a public school founded in 1611, singing about giant hogweed, Willow Farms, Scottish rivers and Puerto Ricans stuck in a parallel universe, would still be around, on and off, 55 years later.

Yet there they were, with two of the original founding members now white-haired and optically challenged, and the new-boy lead singer, who joined only 51 years ago, performing sitting down because of several spinal surgeries and a dragging foot. Meanwhile, guitarist Steve Hackett, who left the band in 1977, has been doing very well thank-you, filling halls across the world playing music the band recorded back in the early 1970s, along with choice cuts from his huge solo catalogue. Having been to his shows, and seen grown men cry as they bellow along with 'Supper's Ready', it's clear the music still means a lot to a small but select and, luckily, fairly well-off group of people.

It may be hard to believe, given their later phenomenal commercial success, but Genesis were not very popular at the start of 1972. Certainly not in the UK, anyway. Their third album, *Nursery Cryme* – the first with new boys Hackett and Collins – limped to an embarrassing number 39 in the album charts. Critics blasted the album as confused and pretentious, taking particular aim at the 'godawful' production – 'a murky, distant stew that at best bubbles quietly when what is desperately needed are the explosions of drums and guitars, the screaming of the organ, the abrasive rasp of vocal cords', complained Richard Cromelin in *Rolling Stone* magazine. Even the record company didn't seem to like it, and both Banks and Collins have dismissed it with the withering putdown, 'it's not our favourite'.

True, they were big in parts of continental Europe, particularly in Italy, where the album rocketed to number four and a sellout tour drew crowds of cheering fans. It's probably fair to say that without the Italian success, Genesis would be little more than an obscure question in a very tough music quiz. Even then, an exhausted Steve Hackett considered quitting on his return to Blighty. So their fourth album was make or break time. Popularity in Italy was all very well, but their record label Charisma was based in London and tended to judge its acts by how they performed in the UK, not in Europe. Genesis needed to release something that proved the record label's faith in them.

The seeds of future success had already been sown, thanks to Hackett. Get a Mellotron, he told keyboard player Banks. King Crimson are selling the one they used on *In the Court of the Crimson King*. ('Mind you', Hackett told *Prog* magazine in 2016, 'Robert Fripp had three and I'm sure he said that about all of them'). In conversation with the author, he added: 'I saw what a Mellotron had done for bands such as Crimson and the Moody Blues and I thought, this band needs to sound like an orchestra at times, so it didn't sound just like another rock band'.

Certainly, the founding members of Genesis were unlike most members of other rock bands. Gabriel, Banks, Rutherford and Ant Phillips were shy, uptight public schoolboys from well-off families who shunned the spotlight and initially just wanted other artists to record their twee, ethereal little songs. In his biography, *A Genesis in My Bed* (Wymer Publishing, 2020), rough-edged Londoner Hackett revealed his unease at being asked to 'board a spaceship to a new planet with a bunch of aliens'.

Thankfully, the other new boy, Phil Collins, was a different breed, another Londoner with a background as a child actor and a cheeky chappie persona capable of cutting through the fog of uncomfortable non-communication that seemed to surround the founder members. In his autobiography, *Not Dead Yet*, he wrote:

> It will take me a while to understand these dynamics. Tony and Peter, for example, are the best of friends, and the worst of enemies. Tony is prone to losing his temper, but this only makes itself apparent later, with Peter and Tony taking it in turns to storm out of the studios in a huff. Mike keeps a delicate balance between the two. But all three of them are what they are: ex-public schoolboys, with all the privilege and baggage that comes with that sort of background. Immaculately bred as officers and gentlemen for a bygone age – perhaps less obvious fodder for a rock group emerging from the tumult of the swinging Sixties.

With two unsuccessful albums behind them and a third that showed promise but failed to perform in the UK, it would take a brave man to bet on this disparate crew to become one of the biggest pop acts of the 1980s, let alone create, within the next few months, one of the classics of progressive rock. There is certainly no suggestion that the members of Genesis felt any pressure to come up with the goods. They had three weeks at a country manor to compose and rehearse for *Nursery Cryme*. But in the run-up to *Foxtrot*, they were gigging practically constantly at the end of 1971 and through the following year, so they had to snatch moments on the tour bus or in dressing rooms or on rare days off to come up with new material. Hackett told me: 'We did it on the run. You would have an idea at an airport, a riff that was hanging around a bit, and you would have to find a spare moment to develop it. You would have other ideas and then join them up later'.

Trundling through the UK, Belgium, Italy and France, it was not difficult for guitarist Hackett or bassist Rutherford to pick up an acoustic guitar and strum out some ideas on the back seats of the tour van. Harder for Banks to find space for his Mellotron, so many of his ideas came about during soundchecks. Eventually, the band found some rehearsal time and space in the unlikely setting of a basement at the Una Billings School for Dance in Shepherds Bush, London, developing and honing the various musical ideas each member brought to the party to the sound of enthusiastic feet clomping through the ceiling. Perhaps that's where the rhythm for 'Watcher of the Skies' came from.

Or perhaps not, because 'Watcher' was one of two *Foxtrot* tracks that took shape on tour and were premiered live long before the album was recorded, opening the show as early as April 1972. It clearly came about through Banks trying out various chord shapes and accompanying bass notes during soundchecks, suddenly hitting on something that sounded like nothing he had ever heard before. Banks and Rutherford wrote the lyrics on the roof of a building during a soundcheck for the show in Naples, dating it exactly to 19 April. Their inspiration was typically public school snobbery – an 1817 poem by John Keats called 'On First Looking Into Chapman's Homer', itself inspired by reading George Chapman's 1611 translation of Homer's Iliad. One of the couplets said, 'Then I felt like some watcher of the skies/When a new planet swims into his ken'.

But the track didn't really take off until Collins supplied the staccato beat beneath it – what Hackett described to me as 'almost bebop meets Morse Code'. He added: 'The rhythm was very clever, but it wasn't doing what normal rhythms do, which is to make it swing'. In fact, the rhythm is so complicated that the late, great John Wetton was unable to play bass and sing at the same time when he performed it with Hackett's band many years later. This is not a slur on the King Crimson legend, who usually took tricky-dicky time signatures in his stride. There aren't too many singing bass players who could pull it off.

The second track to get an early live outing was 'Can-Utility and the Coastliners', mostly written by Hackett and unveiled to unsuspecting audiences in early April, even before 'Watcher'. Hackett developed the opening circle of chords that shift from D major to B major and then back again while sharing musical ideas with ex-King Crimson member Ian McDonald, then wrote the lyrics based on the story of King Canute attempting to command the waves.

In early live performances, it variously went by the names 'Bye Bye Johnny' or 'Rock My Baby' and could last for close to 10 minutes – there's a particularly ropey bootleg recording from Verona in Italy on 9 April that sticks fairly close to the later recording, except that the structure of the second half of the song has not been nailed down yet, introducing new lyrics that were later dropped. The band worked with Hackett on the frantic, chord-shifting ending – Tony Banks supplying an extraordinary Mellotron section of fast arpeggios, Collins improvising on drums and Rutherford coming up with a rich bass pedal sound to anchor it – and a little overlooked gem was created that was to close side one of the album. Later, Hackett visited the Marquee music venue in London and heard some music coming out of the speakers. 'That sounds great! What is it?' he asked. He was told: 'That's you guys...' It was the end section of 'Can-Utility', sounding as fresh and exciting as the day they recorded it.

Hackett's other standalone offering for the album was a criminally-short acoustic guitar melody that has since become a bit of a calling card for him – rare is the concert in which he doesn't perform it. Introduced with tinkling harmonics, it owes a little something to Paul McCartney's 'Blackbird' and also to Mauro Giuliani's 'Raccolta No.6 Andante in C' (although 'Horizons' is in G), better known as the theme for the children's TV programme, 'Tales of The Riverbank'. Hackett, though, credits Bach as an inspiration. For the recording on *Foxtrot*, he put his acoustic guitar through a Leslie cabinet – an amplifier developed in the 1930s that rotates a drum or baffle in front of the speaker to give it a swirly sound reminiscent of a pipe organ.

Other tracks on the album made their first appearance when the band started rehearsals during a break in touring. Banks came in with 'Time Table' and basically said, 'that's it'. A relatively simple piano ballad, it is seen as the missing link between *Nursery Cryme* and *Foxtrot* as it could have sat perfectly happily on the former album, along with similar songs such as 'For Absent Friends' and 'Harlequin'. It's mostly all piano – Hackett is on there but providing an underplayed arpeggio figure.

The subject matter is similar to Percy Bysshe Shelley's poem 'Ozymandias' – the ephemeral, fleeting nature of 'greatness' and 'power'. The 'Time Table' – two words, pedantry fans – is literally that: an old table, dating back to Tudor times or before, perhaps seen by Banks in a stately home or manor during the band's travels across the UK. Carved into the table are the marks of kings and queens from the distant past who thought they were all-powerful but now are just names in dusty history books. Only the rats hold sway now. This leads into a hippy-dippy chorus that is still true despite being a bit of a cliche: 'Why do we suffer each race to believe that no race has been grander?' Whether it's manifest destiny or Brexit, the ability of various races to fool themselves with delusions of grandeur remains undiminished.

Opening with a baroque flourish, 'Time Table' is a pleasant, medium-paced song that is inevitably dwarfed by the bigger beasts around it on side one. It ends with a gentle tune that cleverly changes key as it fades away, with some lovely, lyrical bass playing from Rutherford.

The final side one track to mention is 'Get 'Em Out By Friday', one of the band's story songs in a similar vein to 'Harold the Barrel', 'The Fountain of Salmacis' and 'The Battle of Epping Forest', in which Peter Gabriel sings from the viewpoint of different characters. In this instance, he is John Pebble of property developers Styx Enterprises, who needs to shift residents out of their homes in Harlow so he can demolish them for flats; Pebble's employee Mark Hall, known as The Winkler for his ability to 'winkle' people out of their much-loved properties; Mrs Barrow, a tenant who is forced to move; a TV announcer in 2012 (which, in 1972, was some distant time in the future!); Joe Ordinary in his local puborama (a pub with TV screens – nah, that will never catch on); Sir John De Pebble of United Blacksprings International (who may be a future version of John Pebble, having been knighted no doubt thanks to his contributions to the Tory party); and, finally, Satin Peter of Rock Developments Ltd – the 'Satin' being a deliberate misspelling of 'Saint' to make it close to 'Satan'.

According to author Durrell Bowman, the story was 'inspired by issues Gabriel and his [then] wife were having with the landlord of their flat in London's Notting Hill. In particular, he wouldn't fix the holes in the bathroom and/or kitchen ceilings. The song's story, though, is vaguely based on actual modernist tenant blocks that were built in Northwest Harlow in the 1950s. It can also be seen as a reference to the notorious 1950s landlord and brothel-keeper Peter Rachman, who bought up properties across London and subdivided them to rent out to migrant families, charging them massively over-inflated amounts to live in what was essentially slum accommodation.

The song cleverly matches musical moods to the characters – a frantic opening to illustrate John Pebbles' determination to get things done, an insidious, beguiling melody for the Winkler to slither in and use his persuasive skills and a gentle, wistful section for poor Mrs Barrow to lament the changes being forced upon her. Halfway through, the song almost slows to a halt as we get a 'time passing' section; Gabriel plays a slow, slightly menacing melody on his flute over repetitive five-note bass backing. We are now in the almost unimaginable future of 2012 when Genetic Control announces a four-foot restriction on humanoid height. Then we go into the frantic section again as the story repeats itself – 'now that people will be shorter in height, they can fit twice as many in the same building site'. It's time for The Winkler to work some more.

It ends with a final blast of cynicism, a statement from 'Satin Peter' who is now a mouthpiece for big business providing divine approval for nefarious property dealings. Anyone who finds this offensive should remember that, certainly in England, the role of the Church has been to provide succour and support to capitalism and give God's blessing on keeping the poor in their place. Indeed, the Church of England is one of the nation's biggest landowners, with a property portfolio worth £2 billion. The last thing they want is the poor getting their hands on it.

It's a rare blast of social realism from a band that usually sang about myths and legends, but it would not be the last time Genesis would step out of their literary comfort zone – the title of their 1973 album, *Selling England By The Pound*, and the song 'Dancing With the Moonlight Knight', were both inspired by the 1973 economic crisis and the rise of consumerism.

We come, finally, to the track upon which *Foxtrot*'s reputation and longevity stands: the 23-minute 'Supper's Ready'. Frequently voted the best epic prog rock song of all time, even Tony Banks – who has been dismissive of the band's progressive rock past – admits it was probably their peak, and, curmudgeonly, Gabriel has been known to acknowledge its strengths. In 2017, he told *Prog* magazine:

It does feel like we captured some emotion there, particularly at the climax. For my part, it was influenced by John Bunyan's *The Pilgrim's Progress*, as, later, was *The Lamb Lies Down on Broadway*. It was that idea of a journey. Also, we were then trying, consciously, to break out of tradition. We were tossing together different ideas and influences to see if there was a fresh way of putting them all together. I still enjoy it now; I'm still attracted to it.

It is clear from the track's fragmented nature that it didn't start out as one long piece but, instead, was a series of separate musical ideas shoehorned together, rather like the medley on The Beatles' *Abbey Road* album. Some of the sections date back to Tony Banks's university years, but others were spontaneously created during rehearsals at the Una Billings Dance Studio. Some musical ideas do make a reappearance in other places, and the finale is a deliberate reworking of an earlier section, but others seem to drop in from nowhere and leave without a backward glance. This fragmentation is accentuated by the decision to separate the sections into seven named parts on the lyric sheet (unlike *Thick as a Brick*, for example, which had to wait until it was 40 years old to get subtitles). Hackett claims some influence over the decision to attempt knitting the pieces together. He told me:

I remember saying to the band, having seen King Crimson live in 1969 before they produced that extraordinary album, they were closing their show by segueing three or four different pieces together. It went down very well with audiences, and of course, they had a very sophisticated light show at the time. I said to Genesis, I think we can do a long-form piece, I think we can get away with it, but we do need all the bells and whistles. You do need sounds and light with it, you do need that synchronicity. The music played to audiences in 1972 without a light show just had them going off to the bar in droves until we had a light show and a lead singer who was prepared to live the songs and depict the action. A bit of theatre, even if at times, it blurred into pantomime, something that made the more difficult music more palatable, more digestible.

To be fair, it wasn't the first time Genesis had attempted a multi-sectioned beast, and 'Supper's Ready' was initially seen as a follow-up to 'The Musical Box' on Nursery Cryme. Indeed, both tracks have very similar, low-key openings, with mysterious, tinkling twelve-strings shifting through minor and major keys, and dense, slightly menacing lyrics evoking dark, dangerous nursery rhymes. Unlike 'The Musical Box', 'Supper's Ready' has no intro – voice and guitar kick things off together (with an Am6 chord if you want to try it at home), but the atmosphere is the same.

There's the repetitive phrase of 'Hey my baby don't you know our love is true' that echoes 'Play me my song, here it comes again', and both have a mournful minor key instrumental led by Gabriel's flute, before a gentle linking section with child-like lyrics – 'Old King Cole was a merry old soul' in the earlier song, 'I know a farmer who looks after the farm' in the latter. The lyrics are as mysterious as the music, supposedly inspired by supernatural events experienced by Gabriel and his wife, with the singer 'walking across the sitting room' and seeing ghostly figures moving across his lawn.

Both serve to lull the listener into a false sense of security before being rocked out of their stupor by a sound explosion – in 'The Musical Box', it's two power chords with stabbing organ over the top; in 'Supper's Ready', a sudden shift to a major key for the anthemic 'Guaranteed Eternal Sanctuary Man'. And both go back to a sombre interlude before a final climax – 'She's a lady, she's got time' and 'Wandering in the chaos the battle has left'. But then the tracks diverge, thanks to 'Willow Farm'.

It was a quirky little song penned by Gabriel, obliquely referencing how the mind can be locked into extremes – left and right, up and down, good and bad – but is also packed with bizarre, almost Python-esque imagery and Goonish wordplay of butterflies, flutterbyes, butterflies, Winston Churchill in drag, the frog that's a prince, that's a brick, that's an egg, that's a bird. Hadn't you heard? There is also the reference to a fox on the rocks that was to inspire the album's name and cover art, plus a nod to 'The Musical Box'. In a 1972 concert program, Gabriel explained that the lovers in the song are 'right in the middle of a myriad of bright colours, filled with all manner of objects, plants, animals and humans. Life flows freely and everything is mindlessly busy'. Adding 'Willow Farm' to the mix, introduced by four descending chords, created something that made 'The Musical Box' sound mundane. Banks told *Prog* magazine:

We thought, what if we suddenly went from there into this 'ugly', descending-chords sequence? Nobody would be expecting that. That then brought in all the louder, electric instruments, and once we got into that... well, we were there now, so let's carry on! With freedom. See where that leads us. When we put the whole thing together and heard it back for the first time, we went: 'Oh, this is actually pretty good'.

There was one more new section to come that took the band into even heavier rock territory. Collins recalled in his autobiography:

I am absent from Una Billings for a few hours one day, and when I return, Tony, Mike and Steve have messed around with a riff in 9/8. I haven't a clue what is happening and just start to play. At some points, I play with the riff; at others, I join Tony. I'm still immensely proud of the final recorded performance of the piece, which became Apocalypse in 9/8, which captures me making it up as I go along.

Initially thought of as an instrumental, Gabriel wrote some lyrics to go with it, which 'pissed off' Banks. But he later admitted to *Prog* magazine: 'Then I realised it now had all the excitement we'd been hoping to create. Especially the '666' bit. There's a lot of drama in the chords themselves, but then what he did on top just took it to another level. That half-minute or so is probably our peak'.

It certainly demolished the belief in some quarters that Genesis were an airy-fairy band churning out twee twelve-string instrumentals. This was more like Magma during their most uncompromising moments; a pounding, rocking, exciting piece of menacing prog guaranteed to blow the cones out of your speakers.

After that, it was a straightforward matter of reprising the 'Hey babe' section from part one, and then the triumphant melody from part two, the 'Guaranteed Eternal Sanctuary Man', with its upbeat and suspiciously religious lyrics about the 'Lord of Lords, King of Kings' returning to lead his children home to a new Jerusalem. Gabriel admits it was inspired by Revelation in the Bible and also by King Crimson's lyricist Peter Sinfield's spiritual psychedelic visions. And the reference to the 'new Jerusalem' clearly comes from poet William Blake's writings that suggested Jesus Christ visited England and established a new spiritual centre there.

The track was recorded in separate individual sections rather than as one long piece at the insistence of producer David Hitchcock, who believed this would allow the band to concentrate on the correct instrumentation and approach to each part. It was the first time Hitchcock had worked with Genesis, who had some difficulty finding engineers and producers for *Foxtrot*. John Anthony had produced *Nursery Cryme* and non-album single 'Happy the Man', but there were disagreements with record label Charisma over costs. Recording had begun with Lindisfarne and Van Der Graaf Generator producer Bob Potter on the faders, but he didn't like the music. Eventually, the band settled with Hitchcock and engineer John Burns, who produced the next three albums.

At first, Genesis feared they had made a big mistake with 'Supper's Ready'. Hackett thought it was too long and ambiguous and audiences would never buy it. He expected Charisma boss Tony Stratton-Smith to cancel their contract. Instead, Smith was over the moon, believing the band had finally fulfilled its artistic promise, saying of the album: 'This is the one that makes their career'.

For once, a record label boss was proved right. *Foxtrot* was hailed as the best album the band had so far produced. Jerry Gilbert of *Sounds* magazine said the band had created 'almost the perfect album'. Chris Welch of *Melody Maker* decided it was 'a milestone in the group's career'. It regularly appears in 'best of' lists – *Rolling Stone* magazine puts it at number fourteen in the 50 Greatest Progressive Albums.

For Genesis, it was the beginning of so many things, including the eventual departure of Peter Gabriel. Donning his wife's dress and a fox's head on stage, and introducing songs with obscure, rambling stories, Gabriel became the public image of the band, particularly in the musical press, probably accelerating his move to becoming a solo artist.

Genesis played 'Supper's Ready' in concert almost non-stop until the late 1970s when it no longer fitted the band's new commercial, chart-topping approach. But Hackett resurrected it in 2012 for his second Genesis Revisited album and, from then on, performed it fairly regularly, with Nad Sylvan taking the vocal duties. Today, it ranks alongside 'Close to the Edge' as a classic example of the prog epic, and one that packs as much of an emotional and musical punch as it did 50 years ago.

Yes – *Close to the Edge*

Personnel
Jon Anderson: lead vocals
Bill Bruford: drums, percussion
Steve Howe: guitar, electric sitar, backing vocals
Chris Squire: bass, backing vocals
Rick Wakeman: keyboards
Recorded February to June 1972 at Advision Studios, London
Produced by Eddy Offord and Yes
Engineered by Eddy Offord
Label: Atlantic
Released date: 13 September
Chart placings: UK: 4, US: 3, Holland: 1, Canada: 7
Tracks: 'Close to the Edge' – i) 'The Solid Time of Change', ii) 'Total Mass Retain',
iii) 'I Get Up, I Get Down', iv) 'Seasons of Man' (Anderson, Howe), 'And You
and I' – i) 'Cord of Life', ii) 'Eclipse', iii) 'The Preacher, The Teacher', iv) 'The
Apocalypse' (Anderson, Bruford, Squire, Howe), 'Siberian Khatru' (Anderson,
Howe, Wakeman)

The story so far...

The band was formed in London in 1968 by Jon Anderson, Chris Squire, Bill
Bruford, guitarist Peter Banks and keyboard player Tony Kaye to play original
songs and souped-up cover versions that emphasised their arranging abilities.
Signed to Atlantic Records, their self-named debut album failed to make the
charts. Follow-up, *Time and a Word*, recorded with an orchestra, reached
number 45 in the UK but led to the departure of Banks, who disagreed
with musical direction. Replacement Steve Howe came from the psychedelic
rock group Tomorrow, and his string-based versatility and composing chops
helped the band produce *The Yes Album* in 1971, which hit number four in
the UK and number 40 in the US. Friction between Howe and Kaye led to the
latter being fired, replaced by classically trained Rick Wakeman, who had just
left The Strawbs. Fourth album *Fragile* played on the strengths of the band
and showed the way forward with the multi-part track 'Heart of the Sunrise'.

The album

Yes were close to the edge when they made *Close to the Edge*. That's where
the name came from. For Bruford, it was enough to drive him over the edge.
   In the 50 years since the album's release, the band has skated close to
the edge on many occasions and quite a few people have plunged over
the edge into the abyss – or, like Rick Wakeman, joined, left, rejoined, left,
rejoined, left, rejoined, left, rejoined and, finally, left. For good. Possibly. By
my reckoning, nearly 20 musicians have come and gone – the current line-up
features nobody from the debut album and just one member, Steve Howe,

who predates 1980. This has led to some fans complaining that 'it's not really Yes', the authenticity of membership being a somewhat prog preoccupation. After all, no one says it's not really the London Symphony Orchestra because nobody is still there from the original 1904 line-up.

But I digress. The 1972 incarnation is considered classic Yes, even though it lasted for just two albums (three if you include drummer Alan White, four if we throw *Going For the One* into the mix). For most progressive rock fans, *Close to the Edge* is the band's pinnacle, 38 minutes of pure magic when everything was in balance, the yin and yang of the band blending in perfect harmony. Yes can be seen as pompous, impenetrable and overblown, but on *Close to the Edge,* the pomposity was balanced by passion, the impenetrability by glorious, catchy melodies and the overblownery, if there is such a word, by moments of gentle, sparse beauty.

It was the band's fifth album, but, in many ways, one could look at it as the third. Those first two attempts were the work of five musicians groping towards something, and discovering they needed to make a few personnel changes along the way to reach their ultimate goal. What came through most strongly were their arranging skills, their ability to take a simple pop song and expand it into something that was almost cinematic – or, in the case of 'No Opportunity Necessary, No Experience Needed', add cinematic elements to an original song to create something big and impressive. Working with an orchestra may have alienated Peter Banks, but it was all part of Yes's ambition to make big music – to explore a Big Country, perhaps.

The Yes Album in 1970 was, indeed, *the* Yes album, the one that pointed them in the right direction and lit the blue touch paper. Practically every song on the LP was a cracker and has remained part of the live repertoire. *Fragile,* in 1971, gave each member a chance to shine – particularly keyboard wizard Wakeman, who was fresh out of The Strawbs and David Bowie's backing band. But the track that pointed the way to the future, that excited the band with its possibilities, was 'Heart of the Sunrise'.

Credited to Anderson, Squire and Bruford (but with important contributions from Wakeman), it is nearly eleven minutes of shifting, changing music in a variety of keys and time signatures, clearly pieced together from a number of separate ideas. Squire contributed the three-and-a-half minute introductory riff that owes more than a little to the instrumental section in King Crimson's '21st Century Schizoid Man'; Anderson, the pretty vocal melodies; Bruford, the powerful, inventive drumming that holds everything together; Wakeman, the various classical piano and Mellotron flourishes (he couldn't be credited because of contractual issues but the record company promised him additional money that he says he never saw).

Taking up half of side two of *Fragile,* 'Heart of the Sunrise' showed Yes could create long-form pieces that not only held the listener's attention but could also be played live on stage. Bruford said in his 2009 autobiography: 'Until 'Heart of the Sunrise', we were a covers band trying to be a progressive rock group and not quite knowing how'. So it seemed a short hop to go from nearly eleven minutes to nineteen with the title track of *Close to the Edge*. Again, Bruford's book provides us with a witty commentary on its origins that deserves to be repeated word for word:

> Bands were competing on excess in all areas, from studio time consumed to the power of your PA systems, from the length of guitar solos to the length of your bar bill, from the number of trucks on the road to the number of guitars on stage. In that general spirit, we thought it would be 'fun' to have one track last the whole side of a long-playing vinyl album, which meant about 20 minutes. This was, understandably, an unheard-of feat [although it wasn't really. See introduction]; perfect, then, for our little ensemble.

Like Genesis after them, Yes chose the unusual surroundings of the Una Billings Dance School to start rehearsals following a short break after the *Fragile* tour. The band was keyed up and full of energy, buoyed by the rapturous reception given to the long songs in the set. Surely, recording *Close to the Edge* was going to be a breeze.

It turned out to be a little more challenging than expected. For a start, they kept forgetting what they had done the day before. Even when they moved to Advision Studios to begin recording, they could barely play the first few minutes of the long song all the way through. They had to sift through rehearsal tapes to find the sections they liked and recreate them while the studio clock was ticking. That's if there *was* a rehearsal tape ...

Jon Anderson, in a 2021 interview with Neal Morse, recalls: 'I wanted an intro, you know, and the guys had been jamming away. I remember walking in and this jam was happening and I said, "Are we recording this? We're not? Why not?!!??"'

The composing process was dominated by Anderson and Howe, leaving the other three to sit around twiddling their thumbs or making intricate sculptures out of paperclips until their talents were called upon. Bruford admits: 'I behaved badly, larking about, bored. I would have killed for a decision on anything, but multi-track recording and the deft editing work of our engineer, Eddy Offord, ensured that all decisions could be postponed, seemingly indefinitely'. The most useful judge of what the band was creating turned out to be the cleaning lady – as she wiped up around them late at night, she would be asked her opinion because none of the band could decide.

Every completed section would be discussed and dissected, every instrument subject to analysis, every note up for democratic vote. With Anderson and Howe leading the way but trying hard not to appear to do so, the recording and assembling of the three tracks that make up the album became a long, tortuous process. Bruford said: 'It was horrible, it was incredibly unpleasant and unbelievably hard work'.

Even when the band did decide on something, did say yes, that's the three or four seconds we can all agree on, pernicious Fate intervened. Bruford recalls a time when they all agreed they should go with Edit Section 1(b) v2 Sec 7, only to discover to their horror, that it wasn't there! It was gone! Who saw it last? The cleaning lady! The tape was found with not too much muck on it in a dustbin outside the studio.

The fact that out of this chaos, confusion and indecision came such musical genius is partly down to the talents of the performers but also to Eddy Offord's wizardry with a razor blade and a clearly prodigious memory. Anderson and Howe may have had a cunning plan but, to this day, Bruford and Wakeman are still not entirely sure how they eventually got there. 'Close to the Edge' seemed to come together despite the band's best efforts to make the process as complicated and unpleasant as possible. Here's Rick in *Prog* magazine 2022:

It's almost 50 years old, and I don't know, technically, how the hell we made that album. We did things that really we shouldn't be able to do technically. I think it was the last album made, in my view, where technology was way behind what musicians wanted to do, certainly with us. So to me, it's a very, very special album. And I think it was during the period of time when the band was at one of its peaks; everyone was playing really well.

Talk to Jon Anderson, however, and you get a different impression – according to him, everything was plain sailing, with the vocalist acting as a master of ceremonies or an orchestral conductor, drawing music out of the ether with his baton, and occasionally pointing it at a band member and demanding an immediate contribution. That jam he spoke about earlier led to the punchy opening of the title track (after a few seconds of ambient, new-agey nature noises inspired by the LP *Sonic Seasonings,* by Walter – now Wendy – Carlos, released in early 1972). In the interview with Neal Morse, he recalls telling the band:

I thought the vibe you were playing before was full of charging energy – dahh da-da-da-da, dahhh da-da-da-da-da-da. What I want you to do is to come in like you're halfway through it – and they looked at me and Bill said, what do you mean? I said, come in like you're ha-na-na-na, ha-na-na-na, da-na-la-la-la – like that! Okay, what key? I said I don't care! Then you need to stop in the middle, and Bill said, why? 'Cos I'm going to put in a vocal thing that goes ahhhhhhhhhh – then da-da-da-da-da. They said, when do you want to stop? I said, well, actually, I have a tape recording of Steve playing this diddly-duh, diddly-duh, diddly-duh, diddly-duh – you were playing it yesterday, do you remember? – and you stop there, Bill. Okay, Jon!

As you can see, it's difficult to understand what the others were complaining about. But what Anderson described above is the dramatic opening to part one of the title track, subtitled 'The Solid Time of Change' (btw, don't read too much into the titles; Bruford asked what 'Total Mass Retain' meant and Anderson had no idea, he had to come up with something quickly). It does indeed sound like the band are in the middle of a fast and furious instrumental section, and we have just dropped in on rehearsals. If it's in any key at all, then it's probably D minor, but most of it sounds like atonal jamming, with Wakeman, Howe and Squire improvising like mad while Bruford holds it together by the skin of his teeth and his snare drum. Think the Mahavishnu Orchestra but in an apparent state of mass panic. So you get a good three minutes of seemingly chaotic music before the band settles into the rhythm for the vocals.

Lyrically, it's typical Jon Anderson, part poetry, part spiritual imagery, part imaginative word salad. He would claim it's all metaphors, but the best thing to do with Anderson's lyrics, not just on *Close to the Edge* but on practically every Yes album, is not to search for meaning but to just enjoy the sounds they make as if they are another instrument in the band. 'A seasoned witch could call you from the depths of your disgrace', he sings, 'And rearrange your liver to the solid mental grace'. Yes, your liver. If it helps, the rest of the band didn't know what he was singing about, either.

As we progress through the track, we are treated to some absolutely beautiful guitar phrases from Steve Howe – I mentioned the Mahavishnu Orchestra earlier but listen to Howe's tone and phrasing on 'Close to the Edge' and tell me if they don't scream John McLaughlin. Not that he's copying or anything, but in the way the stately phrases pierce through your ears like musical arrows. He also embellishes the sound with his Coral electric sitar, made by the Danelectro company and sporting thirteen drone strings that resonate in sympathy with the usual six. It was a cheap and quick way to get that sitar sound that swept popular music in 1966-1967, without the many years of finger-shredding practice that would normally be required.

Anderson composed most of the vocal themes, but the chorus came from a Howe composition called 'The Longest Day of the Year' – we're close to the edge, down by a river, because Howe was living next to the Thames at the time. And we get an early listen to the 'I get up, I get down' phrase, during which the melody goes up on 'up' and, yes, down on 'down'. It's at this point that we plunge into part two, the aforementioned 'Total Mass Retain', although the parts are not as clearly defined on 'Close to the Edge' as they are on, say, 'Supper's Ready'. If it helps, later issues of the album include a single edit of 'TMR' that suggests where the band thought it started – it was issued as the B-side of the reworking of the Simon and Garfunkel song, 'America'.

'TMR' takes us back to the verse melody, with Squire supplying seemingly random pumps of meaty bass guitar before it transforms into a pretty melody based on D, G and G minor, with some almost funky guitar beneath it. On the *Yesworld* website, Anderson explains: 'This part flows. It shows you that you have to let the music guide you. It's best to open up and not force the situation. Everything will come to you'.

By the time we get to part three, we've had close to ten minutes of mostly continuous, driving music. Indeed, we may be close to the edge at this point, so it's time to wind things down a bit for a quieter interlude before the big finish. This is the 'I Get Up, I Get Down' section – Anderson explained to Neal Morse:

The song came about because Steve was playing these chords one day, and I started singing, 'Two million people barely satisfy'. It's about the incredible imbalance of the human experience on the planet. The vocals came together nicely. I'm a big fan of The Beach Boys and The Association – such great voices. Steve and I were working on this, and at one point, he said, 'I have this other song...' And I said, 'Well, start singing it'. And he went [sings], 'In her white lace, you could clearly see the lady sadly looking/saying that she'd take the blame for the crucifixion of her own domain... When I heard that, I said, 'Wait. That's going to be perfect! You start singing that with Chris, and then I'll sing my part'. We have an answer-back thing.

It's dominated by Wakeman's simple piano chords, the answer-back singing, Howe's gentle, sustained guitar and the sitar drone laid over it. It's a truly beautiful, magical piece of music and an effective interlude before we crash into the big church organ finale – recorded, by the way, on the pipe organ at St Giles-without-Cripplegate Church in London. It was the second time Wakeman had used the instrument: he wanted a big church organ sound for the track 'Jane Seymour' on his first solo album and St Giles was recommended by a friend. Even better, the vicar had no intention of charging him anything to use it – although it eventually cost £4,000 in donations to church restoration funds. So when Wakeman needed another pipe organ production number, he already had a prior relationship there to call on. No doubt, the restoration funds got another boost. In fact, one wonders why it wasn't renamed St Rick's.

Then we jump into part four, 'Seasons of Man', as Howe reprises a riff from the intro and Wakeman gets his first proper keyboard solo. Back comes Anderson with the verse melody, we get a reprise of 'Total Mass Retain', the 'I get up, I get down' melody, and, finally, the track ends as it began, dissolving into flowing water and tweeting birds.

With so much energy invested in the title track, it's easy to forget there are two more songs on the B-side of the platter that are almost as iconic and have remained part of the live set for the last 50 years. 'And You and I' is another multi-sectioned monster soaking up ten minutes of groove time, opening with a beautiful solo acoustic guitar piece from Howe (in fact, you hear him tuning up in the studio) before moving into what was originally going to be a simple folk song, with Howe strumming D-shaped chords up and down the neck of his acoustic. But, says Anderson, 'soon we decided that it was to be surrounded by very big themes'.

From the gentle acoustic chorus, the song moves into a stately Mellotron melody penned by Wakeman – Anderson said: 'I would always record Rick when he was writing music. He was working on something at the time, and I said, "Let's develop this theme". It felt really good'. Over the top, Howe plays pedal steel guitar, creating the whooping leaps of sound that are as much an important part of the song as the acoustic opening.

We go back to that finger-picking guitar before Howe strums a sort of country-style melody, with Wakeman floating beautifully on top, before another reprise, this time of the pedal steel melody over Wakeman's Mellotron, ending with Anderson crooning the chorus over acoustic guitar. He recalled: 'I remember when we did 'And You and I' at the Spectrum in Philadelphia for the first time. The whole room was so alive with the music we were making – it was really overwhelming – and when we were finished, the audience cheered and clapped for fifteen minutes. I'm not kidding'.

Last but not least – particularly as it was the opening number for the album tour that followed – comes 'Siberian Khatru', originally an acoustic song from Jon with Howe providing the riffs that hold everything together. Anderson originally sang the word 'khatru' without knowing what it meant – it means 'I wish' in Remeni. So, Siberian I Wish. As I said, don't look for meaning in his lyrics!

Howe, in particular, excels in the song as he seems to move effortlessly between three or four different guitars – his pedal steel is in there, along with his electric sitar. Wakeman plays harpsichord on his solo and the ending is inspired by Igor Stravinsky; to push home the link, the band's 1973 live tour opened with Stravinsky's 'Firebird Suite' before crashing into 'Siberian Khatru'.

Preceded by a single showcasing Yes's reworking of 'America', *Close to the Edge* was released to favourable reviews, with *New Musical Express* calling it 'remarkable', *Cashbox* dubbing it 'a recording masterpiece' and the *Lubbock-Avalanche Journal*, no less, saying the title track was 'a virtual sound trip'.

Even now, 50 years later, *Close to the Edge* is seen as a musical milestone, an album that even those who don't like Yes have to grudgingly admit is an almost perfect slice of prog that sounds as fresh and exciting now as it did in 1972. It was also Bill Bruford's swan song for his time in Yes. He said: 'I loved the record, hated making it and was immediately certain I would never try to do that again'.

In retrospect, it was a good job he didn't hang around for the following year's *Tales From Topographic Oceans*, which took the *Close to the Edge* template and quadrupled it. That would have destroyed him completely. It certainly drove Wakeman away for the first of his many resignations and started a pattern that Yes stuck to for the rest of their career – following up great albums with deeply flawed ones that split the band.

But that doesn't change the fact that Yes have made some stunning music throughout their career and *Close to the Edge* is their triumph. Nothing else comes Close.

Emerson, Lake & Palmer – *Trilogy*

Personnel

Keith Emerson: Hammond C3 organ, Steinway piano, zurna (listed as a "Zoukra"), Moog synthesiser III-C, Mini-Moog model D synthesiser

Greg Lake: vocals, bass guitar, electric and acoustic guitars

Carl Palmer: drums, percussion

Recorded October to November 1971, and January 1972 at Advision Studios, London

Produced by Greg Lake

Engineered by Eddy Offord

Label: Island Records

Release date: 3 July 1972

Chart places: UK: 2, US: 5, Japan: 4, Norway: 4, Holland: 4, Canada: 5

Tracks: 'The Endless Enigma (Part 1)', 'Fugue', 'The Endless Enigma (Part 2)', 'From the Beginning', 'The Sheriff', 'Hoedown', 'Trilogy', 'Living Sin', 'Abaddon's Bolero'

All lyrics by Lake. All music by Emerson except 'From the Beginning' by Lake and 'Hoedown' by Aaron Copland.

The story so far...

Yorkshire-born Keith Emerson played in a variety of bands before achieving commercial and critical success with The Nice in 1968. Greg Lake, from Dorset, played in several bands before being invited to join King Crimson, appearing on their influential debut *In the Court of the Crimson King*. The two met each other when The Nice and KC played at the Fillmore West in San Francisco in 1969. Deciding to form a band, they auditioned Brummie Carl Palmer, who had played in the Crazy World of Arthur Brown before forming Atomic Rooster. Their second gig was at the Isle of Wight Festival in front of a 600,000-strong crowd that ended with the band firing off two cannons. Signed by EG Records (who distributed through Island in the UK and Atlantic in the US), their self-titled debut reached number four in the UK and number eighteen in the US, almost immediately establishing the band as a prog rock supergroup. Their follow-up, *Tarkus*, released in 1971, hit number one in the UK. Their third album, a live performance of Modest Mussorgsky's *Pictures at an Exhibition,* followed just four months later and peaked at number three in the UK and number ten in the US.

The album

How do Emerson, Lake & Palmer change a lightbulb? Carl Palmer's karate instructor holds the bulb and the stage crew revolve the entire lighting rig. So went one of the many jokes about one of the most notoriously excessive progressive rock bands ever. Emerson, Lake & Palmer, or ELP (Another joke: How do you spell pretentious? E. L. P.) became the number one target for anyone claiming prog was up its own fundamental orifice. Even John Peel, who had championed so many early prog bands, called them 'a waste of time, talent and electricity'.

But the problem for the naysayers is this: at their best, ELP were brilliant. Those early albums, up to and including *Brain Salad Surgery,* are unrivalled examples of the classical and rock crossover in prog, bursting at the seams with vibrant, exciting and powerful music played with consummate skill and eye-popping showmanship. When they were good, they were damn good and practically no one else could touch them. When they were bad – think *Black Moon* (1992), *In the Hot Seat* (1994) and *Love Beach* (1978), with that horrific cover of the three of them standing there in front of a palm tree backdrop like the bloody Bee Gees – they could be jaw-droppingly awful.

Yes, they set new standards for excess in the music industry, particularly when it came to touring – at one stage, transporting 40 tons of equipment in specially-branded pantechnicons, including a revolving drum kit, a flying grand piano, thirteen different synthesisers, a Persian rug for Lake to stand on and a 70-piece orchestra. But they were one of the few bands at the time that understood the need to put on a visual as well as musical spectacle, and in doing so, they pretty much created theatre rock (and almost bankrupted themselves in the process).

ELP were derided for taking themselves too seriously, and it is true that Emerson had lofty musical ambitions inspired by the great classical composers of the past. But anyone who could stick daggers in his Hammond organ while levitating in the air, playing Hoedown at breakneck speed, clearly had a sense of humour.

It wasn't just the musicianship and showmanship that made the band special. There was also an internal tension resulting from the fact that Mr Emerson, Mr Lake and Mr Palmer were all perfectionists with massive egos who could argue about four bars of music for years, suggesting the band could implode at any time. They also had distinct musical differences, particularly Emerson with his classical pretensions and Lake with his simpler, song-based approach. Their second album, *Tarkus,* almost broke the band up as Lake objected so strongly to the 'self-indulgent' material Emerson was writing. It made them difficult to predict, as their uneven discography shows.

But in 1972, they were riding the crest of a wave, with three albums under their belt that showed their steady progression from prog rock oddities to world-conquering stadium heroes. *Tarkus,* in particular, showed ELP could create side-long epics just as readily as Yes or Jethro Tull, while *Pictures at an Exhibition* displayed their ability to rock the classics like no one before them. A US tour in early 1972 cemented their reputation and helped boost their albums into the charts, as well as providing a number of legendary ELP stories, like the time they helicoptered into a swamp at night in Puerto Rico – the copter went back out with the dead body of someone whose throat had been slit in a botched drug deal.

Then there was the time in Bologna, Italy, when the promoter set off a barrage of powerful fireworks during 'Rondo'. Unfortunately, the frame carrying the fireworks had fallen over, so the rockets whizzed between Emerson's legs and exploded in the middle of the audience. And there was the occasion when Emerson blew off his own thumbnail by setting off a 'pyro-launcher' – glow plugs that heated up gunpowder, sending out a shower of sparks.

Before all this madness, ELP had gone into the studio and recorded what they considered to be their third LP – in their view, *Pictures at an Exhibition* was more of a live bootleg than a proper album. So the name *Trilogy* worked in a number of ways – the third album containing a three-part title track, recorded by a three-piece.

That's them on the cover, which was originally intended to be designed by Salvador Dali, except he wanted $50,000. Instead, design gurus Hipgnosis created a slightly disturbing piece of Pre-Raphaelite artwork showing the three musicians staring moodily to the left, Emerson and Lake's bodies seemingly merging together like Siamese twins, Palmer a little separated on the right. Perhaps that reflected the songwriting partnership between Emerson and Lake, who dominate the credits, with Palmer just getting a nod for 'Hoedown'. It also meant this was the first ELP album to actually show the band's faces on the cover, which wouldn't happen again until *Love Beach*.

Tarkus had been created and mapped out by Emerson with a 'take it or leave it' approach that rankled Lake and Palmer, who considered it self-indulgent. Lake initially told Emerson: 'I can't play that kind of music. If that's what you want to play, then I think you should look for someone else to play it with'. But *Trilogy* was a more collaborative affair, with both Emerson and Lake working together in the brief periods between tours – they share the credits for all but two of the tracks. It is also an album of shorter pieces – the longest, 'The Endless Enigma' suite, clocks in at less than eleven minutes, while 'Living Sin' is a gnat's whisker over three minutes, a mere blink of an eye in ELP terms.

The band also had many more tracks to play with – 24-track recording had just been introduced and, by linking two machines together, the band could double up to 48! That explains why *Trilogy* is laden with overdubs and turned out to be almost impossible to play live, as well as being an absolute bugger to remix in later years.

The album opens with a heartbeat played by Lake on a muted bass string. He had heard 'The Boys in the Band' from Gentle Giant's 1972 album *Octopus* and was captivated by the sound of a spinning coin in the intro. In the liner notes for the 2016 reissue of the album, Lake said: 'I thought that was really clever and that's where I got the idea of the concept of waking up at birth. What would you hear first? A beating heart. Life starting from nothing. Which is the endless enigma, I suppose'. It was an idea that would be borrowed by, among others, Jethro Tull for *A Passion Play* and Pink Floyd for *The Dark Side of the Moon*.

The beating heart does indeed herald 'The Endless Enigma', a two-part suite bisected by Emerson's 'Fugue'. The heartbeat is joined by eerie, spacey synthesiser, then dramatic stabbing piano flourishes, answered by Palmer's bongo beats, rather like the soundtrack of a 1960s TV spy series. Then there's a high-speed section led by Lake's bass, with Emerson's fingers flying all over his Hammond organ before the stately theme introduces Lake's 'choirboy' vocals. Indeed, there is a hymn-like quality to the way the melody moves steadily along, sometimes with Lake singing to an unaccompanied organ.

The track moves into 'Fugue', a beautiful but utterly unpredictable piano solo by Emerson. A fugue is defined as 'a contrapuntal compositional technique in two or more voices' (thanks Wikipedia!), and here it's Emerson's two hands that play contrapuntal, colliding melodies cascading over each other, growing in speed and intensity until we plunge back into Lake's vocal for part two of 'The Endless Enigma'. 'Fugue' was composed by Emerson while on holiday in Denmark on an upright piano hired from a shop next to the home of Hans Christian Andersen. Listen to Palmer here – the recording would be nothing without his intelligent, sympathetic percussion work, sometimes cheeky and delicate, at others, a crashing, pounding wave that drives the track along.

Despite Lake's assertion that the endless enigma is childbirth, the lyrics are generally believed to be a shot at music critics – 'I'm tired of hypocrite freaks', he sings, 'Your words waste and decay. Nothing you say reaches my ears anyway. You never spoke a word of truth'. The title is also likely to have been inspired by Dali, whose 1938 work of the same name is a paranoiac combination of six separate images overlaid on each other: a greyhound lying down, a mythological beast, the face of Cyclops, a mandolin, a dish of fruit on a table and a woman mending a sail. That probably explains why the band wanted him to design the cover before his financial demands put him out of their league.

Trilogy sported ELP's most successful US single, 'From the Beginning' – a track originally written by Lake for King Crimson's debut until Robert Fripp decided it didn't fit. You can see why – it's an acoustic-based number that mixes flamenco flourishes with Crosby, Stills & Nash, and would indeed have been out of place among KC's doom-laden Mellotron sagas. Opening with Lake's solo acoustic guitar playing a wistful A minor ninth chord, it adds electric guitar, bass and very subdued percussion, finally playing out with a flute-like synth solo and occasional spacey whooshes from Emerson.

Lyrically, the song is in somewhat indistinct singer-songwriter territory, with vague lines about apologising to someone for being cruel because they were meant to be here 'from the beginning', but it possesses an appealing melody that helped push it to number 39 in the US singles chart, the band's highest showing (it doesn't appear to have been released in the UK).

From some gentle introspection, we move to one of ELP's 'novelty songs'. *Tarkus* had one – the execrable rock 'n' roll pastiche 'Are You Ready Eddy?'

– and later albums would be let down by similar nonsensical offerings such as 'Benny the Bouncer' on *Brain Salad Surgery* and 'Show Me the Way to Go Home' on *Works Volume 2*. *Trilogy*'s is much better executed, with superb keyboard work from Emerson, but even that cannot disguise that this is a country and western song. Opening with studio chat and laughter, followed by some random percussion from Palmer (you can hear him exclaim 'Shit!' after accidentally hitting the rim of his tom-tom), Lake sings a story about a sheriff hunting the outlaw Josie, who gets the upper hand at the end, over Emerson's busy Hammond organ. In the liner notes, Lake explained:

> We always liked to do one light-hearted comedic song on each record. We had a lot of classical overtones and our music was sometimes considered elitist by critics. We were acutely aware of this and didn't want to come across as smart arses. So we always tried to do one that was kind of funny. Keith played a honky-tonk piano, so it sounded like an old Western movie.

Indeed it does – not only that, it's introduced by a gunshot, just to drive home the cheesy nature of the track. Honky-tonk originally referred to a type of bar in America's Old West during the late nineteenth century that offered country music entertainment. Eventually, it came to describe a type of piano that was frequently out of tune and had tacks driven into the hammers to create a tinny sound that increased the volume, and then the music itself, a form of simple ragtime that emphasised rhythm over melody.

Emerson is not listed as playing a honky-tonk piano on the record sleeve – the only piano mentioned is a Steinway. However, liner notes for Jakko Jakszyk's surround sound remix of the album insist that he was playing his 'other piano, that has tin tacks pushed into the hammers' rather than utilising a clever synth patch.

'The Sheriff' acts as a sort of introduction to the last track on side one of the original vinyl, a frantic version of Aaron Copland's 'Hoedown'. Born in Brooklyn, New York in 1900, Copland is viewed as the 'Dean of American composers', who helped establish American classical music at a time when the country's output was more Tin Pan Alley than Carnegie Hall. 'Hoe-Down', as it was originally titled, is the climax of his 1942 ballet, Rodeo, choreographed by Agnes de Mille. The piece is based on a British fiddle tune called 'Bonaparte's Retreat', composed sometime after Napoleon Bonaparte's disastrous retreat from Moscow in 1812. The first recorded version was by Kentucky violinist William Hamilton Stepp, and it is this tune that forms the basis for 'Hoe-Down'. Copland's version segues into 'Miss McLoed's Reel', originally a Scottish dance tune that made its way into the Irish fiddle repertoire before heading across the Atlantic, where it became a popular piece for beginner violinists. There's also a brief mention of an Irish hornpipe called 'Gilderoy'.

ELP's version goes at about twice the speed of Copland's original, blasting through the 'Bonaparte's Retreat' section as if Napoleon is evacuating at 100mph. Like Copland, he segues into 'Miss McLoed's Reel' before retreating with 'Bonaparte' again, but there are touches of other folk tunes there, including a brief rendition of 'Shortnin' Bread', an American reel from the late nineteenth century that was given words by poet James Whitcomb Riley in 1900.

Where Copland changes the dynamics of the tune, from loud to soft and back again, Emerson and the band plunge through it like a runaway train – towards the end, Emerson is just holding down long notes while Palmer pounds the drums into submission, before ending with staccato chords.

When Jakszyk started remixing 'Hoedown', he discovered the band had tried it at several different speeds – and all the alternate versions existed somewhere on the 48 tracks! He also discovered how Emerson had got such a bright and beefy Hammond organ sound – he had pumped the output through a Marshall stack, so part of it is coming out of a Leslie speaker. What this does is retain the percussive sound of the keys being pressed, something you would normally want to remove, but on Hoedown, adds to the frantic, almost out-of-control nature of the track.

'Hoedown' became a huge live favourite, one of the few tracks on *Trilogy* that could be played on stage, frequently as the opening number. Emerson was a huge Copland fan and was to have even greater success in the UK with the band's version of 'Fanfare For the Common Man'.

Side two of the original LP starts gently enough with a string intro followed by Lake singing angelically over solo piano. The track is 'Trilogy' and, as the title suggests, it is in three parts: a vocal and piano duet in a warm major key, with Emerson's playing building in content and intensity; a faster, driving instrumental section in 5/4, alternating between Bb and B major, with Emerson adding wailing synth lead lines over bass and drums; a jazzy section that darts about through various keys before settling into another vocal contribution from Lake, his voice treated to give it a tinny quality. Section three ends with Emerson playing an astonishing double-tracked lead over drums and bass crashing away in 12/8, coming to a close with a cheesy showbiz ending.

'Living Sin' was chosen as the B-side of the 'From the Beginning' single – over jazzy Hammond organ and shuffling drums, Lake sings in an uncharacteristically guttural style, alternately shouting and muttering. Palmer's busy drums keep things going before a sudden end after just three minutes and eleven seconds.

The album's closer, 'Abaddon's Bolero', gave the band some difficulties when trying to reproduce it live – there are so many overdubs, they needed to play to a backing tape that repeatedly broke down. It was abandoned after a few attempts and was not successfully performed until the 1977 tour with a full orchestra.

Like Ravel's 'Bolero', this track builds and builds, led by Palmer's marching snare drum – unlike a real bolero, it's in 4/4 time instead of 3/4. Keyboard instruments come in and out, one after another, with a flute-like synth patch offering a brief burst of 'The Girl I Left Behind Me', a sixteenth-century British folk song that used to be played as soldiers marched off to war. It continues to build in intensity, with ever-increasing key changes until, after a mind-blowing eight minutes, it thunders to a close with a series of pounding chords. It owes much to Gustav Holst's 'Mars' – it was originally called 'Bellona's Bolero' after the ancient Roman goddess of war, and Abaddon is Hebrew for destruction or doom – and in particular, the reworking that King Crimson did on *In the Wake of Poseidon*, the eleven-minute 'The Devil's Triangle'.

Trilogy was a hit on both sides of the Atlantic for the band, as well as occupying the Danish Top Ten for four consecutive weeks, and was praised for Emerson's growing accomplishment on all manner of keyboards. It is sometimes overlooked, sandwiched between the ground-breaking *Tarkus* and fan-favourite *Brain Salad Surgery*.

But for many people, it is *the* definitive ELP album – not least for Greg Lake. In the liner notes of the surround sound remix, he said:

I am often asked to choose my favourite ELP album, and for obvious reasons, I always find it difficult to come up with an answer. However, I think if I were forced to choose just one record from the catalogue, then it would probably have to be *Trilogy*, and the reason is that this record was made at a time when the band's inspiration and motivation were absolutely on fire, yet at the same time, we had been together long enough to have begun to form our own musical identity.

That identity was never stronger than on *Trilogy* – I mean, even the obligatory comedy track works! They would produce one more great album before beginning a slide towards the creative doldrums. But on *Trilogy*, the band sounded electrifyingly exciting and together, with ideas bursting out like the dancers in a hoedown. This was, without a doubt, one of the greatest progressive rock albums of 1972.

Sadly, Greg and Keith are no longer with us and, at the time of writing, it is Carl Palmer who is keeping the ELP flame burning brightly. So we should leave him with the last word, again from the liner notes:

The title track 'Trilogy', which I still play on stage today with the Carl Palmer ELP Legacy, is still one of the main musical events of the evening. ELP had come close to perfection with 'Abaddon's Bolero'. The humour of the group is apparent in 'The Sheriff', even if you do hear me swearing on the drum intro... I had a great time recording this album. This was an extremely memorable period in my life, and I am sure I can say the same for everyone involved.

Pink Floyd – *Obscured by Clouds*

Personnel
David Gilmour: acoustic, electric and pedal steel guitars, VCS 3 synthesiser, vocals
Nick Mason: drums, percussion
Roger Waters: bass guitar, vocals
Richard Wright: Hammond organ, piano, Farfisa organ, VCS 3 synthesiser, electric piano, vocals
Recorded 23 February to 6 April 1972 at Chateau d'Herouville studios, France
Produced by Pink Floyd
Label: Harvest
Released 2 June 1972
Chart places: UK: 6, Denmark: 3, Netherlands: 3, Italy: 5
Tracks: 'Obscured by Clouds' (Gilmour, Waters), 'When You're In' (Gilmour, Waters, Wright Mason), 'Burning Bridges' (Wright, Waters), 'The Gold It's in The...' (Gilmour, Waters), 'Wot's... Uh the Deal' (Gilmore, Waters), 'Mudmen' (Wright, Gilmour), 'Childhood's End' (Gilmour), 'Free Four' (Waters), 'Stay' (Wright, Waters), 'Absolutely Curtains' (Gilmour, Waters, Wright, Mason)

The story so far...

London architecture students Waters, Mason and Wright, formed The Tea Set in 1963 with fellow students Keith Noble, Clive Metcalfe and guitarist Bob Klose. Noble and Metcalfe left, replaced by Syd Barrett, childhood friend of Waters. RAF technician Chris Dennis was briefly a singer. Klose left, leaving the four-piece of Waters, Mason, Wright and Barrett to rebrand themselves in 1965 as The Pink Floyd Sound.

A performance at the Marquee Club in London interested economics lecturer Peter Jenner, and business partner Andrew King, who became their managers.

The Pink Floyd (they dropped the Sound) became darlings of London's underground music scene before being signed by EMI. Their first singles, 'Arnold Layne' and 'See Emily Play', hit number 20 and number six in the UK singles chart, respectively (despite radio stations banning 'Arnold' over cross-dressing references) and their debut album, *Piper at the Gates of Dawn,* was a Top Ten UK psychedelic hit. Concerns over Barrett's mental health resulted in Pink Floyd (they had dropped the 'The') recruiting Cambridge-born guitarist David Gilmour. Barrett was dumped in early 1968 before their second album, *A Saucerful of Secrets,* which signalled a more space-rock direction. Subsequent singles failed to register, and the band went through a period of releasing uncertain and patchy albums: *More* (1969), *Ummagumma* (1969) and *Atom Heart Mother* (1970). *Meddle* in 1971, with side-long epic 'Echoes', was critically well-received and commercially successful in the UK, Netherlands and Italy but failed to break the US.

The album

I'm not saying *Obscured by Clouds* is Pink Floyd's best album. I'm not even saying it's number two, or three, or four. In fact, you may not see it in a list of the Floyd's Top Ten releases. But what I *am* saying is that it was an important stepping stone to the multi-million selling, fourteen times platinum-ranking, critically-acclaimed behemoth that is *The Dark Side of the Moon*, and 1972 was a pivotal year in the band's fortunes.

Without *Obscured by Clouds*, *The Dark Side of the Moon* may have been completely different. In addition, it's an overlooked album with several good tracks. Well, that's my story and I'm sticking to it.

As the short biography above suggests, Pink Floyd went through some uncertain years after their superb psychedelic debut, marred by a lack of musical direction and a habit of saying yes to anything that came their way. The loss of Barrett was significant as he was their main songwriter as well as a childhood friend of Waters and Gilmour. The guilt they felt for callously abandoning him manifested itself in their later work, particularly 'Shine on You Crazy Diamond' from 1975's *Wish You Were Here*. Another reason for the patchy quality of some of their albums was that they were soundtracks, and their content and quality were dictated by the demands of the narrative of the movies and their directors rather than by the creative impulses of the band.

Pink Floyd were seen as a useful soundtrack band right from the off – in fact, one of their earliest proper recordings, made in October 1966, was a version of their proto-prog classic, 'Interstellar Overdrive', used in a short impressionist documentary film called *San Francisco*. A longer version also turned up in *Tonite Let's All Make Love in London*, released in 1968.

In that year, the band also provided the soundtrack for *The Committee*, a film noir by Hammer horror director Peter Sykes, before being approached by Iranian-born movie maker, Barbet Schroeder, to score his almost-completed drug-fuelled drama *More*. Nick Mason recalled: 'Barbet was an easy man to work with – we were paid £600 each, a substantial sum in 1968, for eight days' work around Christmas. A lot of the moods in the film... were ideally suited to some of the rumblings, squeaks and sound textures we produced on a regular basis night after night'. The resulting album received mixed reviews, although a few of the songs found their way into the band's live repertoire at the time.

Then there was *Zabriskie Point* by celebrated Italian filmmaker Michelangelo Antonioni, an attempt to make a follow-up to his critically acclaimed and commercially successful thriller *Blow Up*. Working with Antonioni was a more frustrating experience as he rejected take after take, forcing the band to re-record and resubmit different pieces in different styles in an attempt to meet his creative vision. Eventually, he resorted to using music from several sources, including The Grateful Dead, The Rolling Stones and Roy Orbison, while Floyd gathered up their rejected compositions for later recycling. One of them, 'The Violent Sequence', later became 'Us and Them' on *The Dark Side of the Moon*.

Fast-forward to 1972 and Schroeder was back with another film project, this time a story about a band of hippies travelling through Papua New Guinea. It was to be called *La Vallee* and Pink Floyd were invited to France to record at Elton John's 'Honky Chateau' for two weeks in February. It was a tight schedule for the band, who also had a number of other important projects, one of which was a new music suite that partly debuted in January at Brighton's Dome but was abandoned halfway through due to technical difficulties.

The two weeks in France, sandwiched between a sixteen-date UK tour in January and their first visit to Japan in March, was interrupted by a camera crew who descended on Chateau d'Herouville and captured a band looking tired and short-tempered. Gilmour and Waters certainly give the impression they resented having to put aside the other project they were working on to score the movie (although Gilmour quite openly mentions the tax advantages of working abroad) and they talk more about their growing political awareness than they do about the music.

In a telling moment, Gilmour says the band won't turn down other soundtracks before Waters interrupts with: 'Unless we finally have our breakdown, of course'. Gilmour says: 'Yes, if we crack up and fall about the floor raving'. Waters then bemoans the fact that they have only had a few days off, adding: 'There's hundreds of people asking you to do things and there's a fantastic temptation to do them all... I still personally think we are accepting too much work'. Ah, the troubles of the poor, overworked rock star.

For *Obscured by Clouds*, the band used the same techniques employed on *More* – watching a rough cut of the film and timing the musical sections with stopwatches. In his entertaining autobiography *Inside Out*, Mason explained:

> Standard rock song construction was optional; one idea could be spun out for an entire section without worrying about the niceties of choruses and middle eights, and any idea in its shortest, most raw version could work without the need to add solos and frills... This method of evolving and modifying themes played to our strengths, but we had no scope for self-indulgence since the recording time available was extremely tight.

They had an opening and closing title to come up with, plus incidental music that needed to reflect the action in the film, in which six people travel to a mysterious valley that is shrouded – or obscured – by clouds on an uncharted island. The result is a collection of pretty tight and succinct songs and instrumentals that rarely break the five-minute mark, the first time Pink Floyd had released an album like that since *More*. And like that album, it shows a heavy side of the band – not as heavy, perhaps, as 'The Nile Song', but the album is certainly dominated by Gilmour's guitar and contains quite a few tracks that rock along nicely. Not all the songs appear in the film – I've had the misfortune of sitting through it and can find no trace of 'Stay' or 'Free Four' or 'Childhood's End' (apart from a brief moment when the travellers strum the opening chords and the main character Vivienne, played by Bulle Ogier, suddenly develops a hitherto unknown talent for playing the bongos).

Remember that Gilmour was not then the guitar god he is now, and 'Obscured' shows a musician really coming into his own. It's probably no coincidence that he also dominates the songwriting credits, making a contribution to seven of the ten tracks, and the singing – Waters was not yet the confident vocalist he would later become.

The two instrumentals that open the album, the title track and 'When You're In', really are little more than a chance for him to wrench lead guitar lines over repetitive chord sequences. Live, they would be segued as one long, fifteen-minute track – indeed, they sound like they belong together on the album as they share the same timing and rhythm, and key of E minor. The title track, on which Mason played a very early set of electronic drums (more like bongos, really), and Gilmour supplied slide guitar over the drone of a VCS-3 synth Wright bought from the BBC Radiophonic Workshop – which would also be utilised in the band's next album – plays over the opening and closing titles of the film. 'When You're In', which ups the energy a notch, was named after a phrase uttered by roadie Chris Adamson.

The first song with vocals is 'Burning Bridges', based on a stately organ melody in 6/4 written by Wright, with Gilmour and Wright singing Waters' lyrics. This is one of only three Waters/Wright Pink Floyd songs and appears in the film when one of the travellers, a bored diplomat's wife, starts drifting away from her old life. The lyrics speak of breaking bonds and escaping from a gilded cage, all fairly standard metaphors, while the key shifts from G major to G minor for the chorus, allowing Gilmour to play haunting slide guitar. The melody is repeated, slightly slower, on piano and in 4/4 time for 'Mudmen' at the end of side one, which is dominated by Wright's keyboards and Gilmour's guitar.

Track four of the album is a fairly straightforward rocker, 'The Gold It's in The...', using mostly alternating chords of E and A – it was the song played for the ORTF TV broadcast on the band working in the studio and was released as the B-side of 'Free Four'. Generally regarded as one of the weakest cuts on the album, it is almost unFloydian in its upbeat, AOR approach.

Luckily, it's followed by one of the strongest songs, albeit again rather atypical of Floyd in that it has a decidedly country flavour. 'Wot's... Uh the Deal?' is an acoustic number played over a particularly fruity scene in the movie when two of the characters make the beast with two backs. With a gentle descending chord sequence and Gilmour's multi-tracked vocals, Waters' lyrics tell of a search for missed opportunities and how your perspective changes with age. Wright provides honky-tonk style piano and Gilmour's lap steel guitar adds to the country rock flavour.

'Childhood's End', which opens side two, is the track that seems to foreshadow the band's future work – it has that same chugging lope as 'Time' on *The Dark Side of the Moon*. Indeed, the opening 'tick-tock' percussion drives home the link even more. The title is said to have come from an Arthur C. Clarke novel about an alien race visiting Earth – the end of childhood is the time when homo sapiens ascend to a higher level, a development that may well be overdue. It's the first track on the album not to appear in the film and the last to feature lyrics by Gilmour – who is the sole songwriter and singer – until the *A Momentary Lapse of Reason* album in 1987. It was released as a single in 2016 to promote a remastered version of the album, accompanied by a video of early Floyd footage. Played live occasionally in 1972 and early 1973, it would frequently get an extended instrumental section.

Waters's only solo composition on the album, and the only one he sings, is 'Free Four', which was released as a single in July 1972. The title comes from the 'one, two, free, four' cockney count-in at the beginning, while the content hints at the writer's future preoccupation with the death of his father, Eric Fletcher Waters, in Italy during World War II. 'I am the dead man's son', sings Roger, 'and he was buried like a mole in a foxhole'. Daddy Waters would later inspire the song 'When the Tigers Broke Free', which appeared in the film adaptation of *The Wall*, and the band's last album with Roger, *The Final Cut*. Played as a jolly singalong in G major, its apparent upbeat nature is belied by the grim subject matter, and instrumental 'choruses' in B major allow Gilmour to provide some scathing guitar.

The penultimate track, 'Stay', is another ballad in a similar vein to 'Wot's... Uh the Deal' which uses a somewhat well-worn folk-rock chord sequence of G, A minor, B minor and C while the bass keeps on G throughout – think Sandy Denny's 'Who Knows Where the Time Goes'. It's credited to Wright/ Waters, but it may well be that Wright wrote not only the tune but most of the lyrics – they cover similar ground as his 'Summer of '68' *from Atom Heart Mother* about reflections on a one-night stand.

Finally, the album ends with a track that *is* from the film: the droning, downbeat instrumental, 'Absolutely Curtains', which plays as the travellers eventually find the cloud-obscured valley. It then segues into some Oceanic chanting by the Mapuga tribe of New Guinea, which actually appears earlier in the film.

The album was going to be given the same name as the movie but, thanks to a last-minute disagreement with the production company, became *Obscured by Clouds* instead. In fact, the film was given that title in parenthesis when it was released (although that is dropped for the version in the *Early Years* box set). The album received mixed reviews, and critics are still divided about its importance and legacy, with some saying it points the way to *The Dark Side of the Moon*, and others dismissing it as a dull soundtrack. But it reached number six in the charts in 1972 and did even better in some other European countries.

As to the film, the less said about that, the better. Slow, detached and almost deliberately undramatic, with emotionless, muttered dialogue and some of the worst acting ever seen on a screen, *La Vallee* failed to match the success of *Blow Up*. It's not even worth watching for Floyd's music because it's all mixed so low, particularly the songs, that they sound like distant broadcasts from a tinny transistor radio.

As to Pink Floyd themselves, they probably weren't terribly concerned about the fate of either the film or the album. They were working on a new suite of songs that they polished up through 1972 and into the following year. When it was released in 1973, it transformed them from an interesting but uneven prog band into critical and commercial monsters of rock.

In 1972, their future was obscured by clouds; in 1973, they had set their controls to the dark side of the moon.

Gentle Giant – *Three Friends & Octopus*

Personnel
Derek Shulman: lead and backing vocals, saxophone
Phil Shulman: saxophone, lead and backing vocals, trumpet, mellophone
Ray Shulman: bass, violin, guitar, backing vocals
Kerry Minnear: Hammond organ, Minimoog, Mellotron, piano, electric piano, harpsichord, clavinet, vibraphone, percussion, lead and backing vocals, cello
Gary Green: guitar, mandolin
Malcolm Mortimore: drums on *Three Friends*
John Weathers: drums, percussion, xylophone on *Octopus*
Three Friends recorded December 1971 at Advision and Command studios
Produced by Gentle Giant
Engineered by Martin Rushant
Label: Vertigo (UK), Columbia (US and Canada)
Release date: 14 April 1972
Chart places: US: 197
Tracks: 'Prologue', 'Schooldays', 'Working All Day', 'Peel the Paint', 'Mister Class and Quality?', 'Three Friends'
All tracks written by Minnear, Shulman, Shulman, Shulman.
Octopus recorded 24 July to 5 August 1972 at Advision and Command studios
Produced by Gentle Giant
Engineered by Martin Rushant
Label: Vertigo (UK), Columbia (US).
Release date: 1 December 1972
Chart places: US: 170
Tracks: 'The Advent of Panurge', 'Raconteur Troubadour', 'A Cry For Everyone', 'Knots', 'The Boys in the Band', 'Dog's Life', 'Think of Me With Kindness', 'River'
All music by Minnear, R. Shulman. All lyrics by D. Shulman, R. Shulman (according to 2015 remix)

The story so far...

The three Shulman brothers were born in the Gorbals, a notorious slum area of Glasgow, Scotland (although, recently, the recipient of much urban regeneration, I hasten to add in case any outraged residents want to nut me). Their dad was a jazz trumpeter who encouraged his sons to learn any instrument they could get their hands on. They put an RnB band together that eventually became Simon Dupree and the Big Sound (Derek was 'Simon') and had an entirely untypical 1967 psychedelic hit, 'Kites' (which they hated). Follow-ups flopped so, in 1969, the brothers changed direction and recruited Dorset-born multi-instrumentalist Kerry Churchill Minnear (yes, Churchill!), who had graduated from the Royal Academy of London; Londoner, Gary Green; and former Dupree drummer Martin Smith. The band's name was a reference to a fictional 'gentle giant' who happens upon a band of musicians, inspired by the writings of Renaissance author Francois Rabelais. Signed to Vertigo, their self-titled 1970 debut was challenging but criticised for poor recording quality. Their 1971 follow-up, *Acquiring the Taste*, showed a further experimental approach, after which Smith left and was replaced by Malcolm Mortimore.

The album

Typical Gentle Giant – almost everyone else gets one album in this book, but GG snaffle two! But then, this was never a band to do things by halves. Just look at all the instruments they played, for a start, particularly the multi-talented Kerry Minnear. Surely, he would have run out of hands.

I could have focussed on one of their 1972 offerings and let the other sit in the corner, unloved and unwanted. But the thing is this: ask a fan for their favourite GG album and they are very likely to opt for *Three Friends*. Ask the critics and they'll point to *Octopus*. So I really have no choice but to offer up both recordings and encourage you, dear reader, to listen and decide.

How to describe Gentle Giant to those who have yet to discover their delights? Let us start by quoting their 'mission statement' in the liner notes of their second album, *Acquiring the Taste* (although producer Tony Visconti has claimed authorship):

> It is our goal to expand the frontiers of contemporary music at the risk of being very unpopular. We have recorded each composition with the one thought – that it should be unique, adventurous and fascinating. It has taken every shred of our combined musical and technical knowledge to achieve this.

Well, they certainly had the musical chops – they played about 46 instruments between them. And they had the ability to craft intricate, complicated compositions drawing on mediaeval and baroque music forms, as well as folk, rhythm and blues and jazz. In fact, practically everything went into the melting pot of the typical Gentle Giant creation – it seems too trivial to call them 'songs' – along with an apparent complete and utter disregard for commercial success (although that changed as time went on). You want progressive? Gentle Giant were way out there, even compared to some of the other prog bands highlighted in this book.

So it may come as some surprise to learn that it took GG until their third release to create a concept album. *Three Friends* was, as the title suggests, the story of three friends growing up together and growing apart – a simple enough concept but one that gave the band a framework around which to construct their complicated music. The concept came out of Derek and Ray talking about old friends in Glasgow and where they were now and how they had changed. Ray said they would do a gig and there in the audience would be a face they vaguely recognised from the past, and then you realised you had been to school with him. In an interview with music director Jeff Pollack, for KCFR College Radio in Denver, Colorado, Derek added: 'Those sort of conversations we thought we would log anyway and put down on an album. And that became *Three Friends*'.

Adding to the challenge was a change of drummers, studios and producers. The band decided Martin Smith's percussion style was too jazzy and poppy for a band that frequently played in time signatures only Albert Einstein would understand, so they auditioned for a replacement. Malcolm Mortimore got the job – in fact, he had no idea who he was auditioning for until he was given the news he was Gentle Giant's new drummer.

The first two releases were made at Trident, AIR and Advision, but this time the band checked into Command Studios in Piccadilly, an unfamiliar environment, to start recording the new album. The musicians also felt they could produce themselves, so dispensed with the services of Tony Visconti, who had helmed the first two albums and took control of the faders. But early sessions were fraught – the band were not experienced enough to get the best results and were relying on the house engineer to know what he was doing.

Then there was the car accident. Derek explained in the liner notes for *Three Piece Suite*, Steven Wilson's remix of tracks from the first three albums :

We were on our way to the studios one day. I was driving. Derek, Kerry and Phill were also in the car. It was on a dual carriageway and it was raining very hard. We had bald tires and went into a skid. The car crossed the carriageway, turned around and landed facing the oncoming traffic. It was a miracle we didn't get hit and that no one got hurt. The incident mirrored our feelings about the start of the album. We felt we were on the wrong path, so we kept some of the basic tracks, abandoned Command Studios and went back to Advision. That made us feel a lot more at home. We knew Advision well and were able to complete the album there.

The opening 'Prologue' sets the scene:

Three friends are made, three lives are laughs and tears
Through years of school and play they share
As time stands still the days change into years
And future comes without a care.
But fate and skill and chances play their part
The wind of change leaves no good-bye
Three boys are men their ways have drawn apart
They tell their tales to justify

The short verses are surrounded by busy music, mostly piano, guitar and synth, showcasing the band's ability to play fast melodic lines that shift and change as the song moves through seemingly unrelated keys but still create

53

drama and not a little suspense. There's a mysterious eight-note motif that repeats itself throughout but in different keys. What's happening? Who are these people? Why should we care about them?

The track slows for the vocals, which feature Phil taking the lead while Minnear and the other Shulmans create a sort of Greek chorus, responding to his words. Then there's a section of repetitive organ lines that build up into heavy, crunching guitar riffs repeating the eight-note motif before fading. If you detect the odd Jethro Tull influence, particularly in the use of the Hammond organ, then that is no surprise, as the band supported Tull on the latter's winter tour before going into the studio.

Second track 'Schooldays', does what it says on the tin and focuses on the carefree days of later childhood – 'Schooldays, the happy days when we were going nowhere'. There's a childlike simplicity – well, simple for Gentle Giant – in the vibraphone and synth intro and the almost nursery rhyme-esque melody line, although, as usual, it is punctuated by little instrumental moments that transpose the song into different keys, including a sneaky reference to 'Ring Around the Rosie' (a song originally about counting rosary beads while praying).

It moves into a dramatic 'time-changing' section, with the piano playing deep chords with the regularity of a ticking clock, before more wistful vocals emerge about friendships changing – 'Remember when we together went to the sea... the days of children gone'. The child's voice you can hear is Phil's son Calvin, then eleven, who was put into a studio recording booth with headphones on and told to sing along with Dad. Amazingly, he did it in one take.

The melodies here are beautiful and affecting and the piano accompaniment is almost classical in its rich chords. Finally, a faster ending section could be the Modern Jazz Quartet as Minnear plays a dazzling vibraphone instrumental to bring the song to a wistful close.

After 'Schooldays' we get three tracks that are dedicated to each of the three friends in their working lives. One has become a road-digger and, in 'Working All Day', he sings about digging for his pay: 'Drown in my sweat but money buys escape. I've got no regrets'. Although, actually, he does because, by the end of the song, he's complaining that the boss is getting all the money and he's going nowhere.

It opens with a little repeated riff that slows down into the main melody line, a swaggering, beefy tune as befits a man scooping up shovel-fulls of road. Phil blows tenor, alto and baritone saxophone to give the song a rough, brassy feel and there's a fairly insistent beat throughout until the end.

Side two opener 'Peel the Paint' has become a fan favourite, mainly because of its three-minute improvised guitar and drums solo from Green and Mortimore. One of the friends has become an artist, and he sings about searching for answers in art. But peel the paint and 'find mad eyes and see those sharpened teeth. Nothing's been learned – No, nothing at all. Don't be fooled, get up before you fall'. There are teeth in the music, too. It starts in a deceptively gentle manner, with string interludes created by Ray's violin multi-tracked many, many times.

But at the 2:30 mark, it erupts into a staccato lead guitar riff by Green – if you detect hints of Martin Barre there, well, I refer you to the reference to Jethro Tull made earlier – and the vocals growl and snarl. For the three-minute improv, Green borrowed an Echoplex from Soft Machine keyboardist Mike Ratledge, while Mortimore was basically told to play whatever he liked – just make a noise. The result is three of the most exciting minutes the band ever committed to tape.

The last of the three character studies, 'Mister Class and Quality?', finds the third friend becoming a white-collar worker – he's in management, in other words – and he seems to have no reservations about his position: 'The world needs steady men like me to give and take the orders' he sings. Opening with a minute of counterpoint melodies on organ, guitar and bass, the song moves into a galloping rhythm for the vocals, with a repetitive violin riff over the top, and an intricate latticework of instrumental melodies. In fact, as GG songs go, this is fairly straightforward as it pretty much finds a groove and stays there, allowing each musician to display his instrumental chops.

The pace doesn't let up until the last verse segues almost imperceptibly into the final track, 'Three Friends' – as Gary Steel, a fellow author in my publisher's stable of wordsmiths, says in his exhaustive examination of the band's output, they go so well together, it's hard to imagine them prised apart. 'Three Friends' wraps things up neatly by suggesting the three friends 'all in gladness, went from class to class' – that is, school class to the British class system. It nods to what went before musically by using the same bass melody that opened the preceding track, and the choir of voices joins the entire group together as an ensemble.

Three Friends can be criticised for its simplistic concept and the fact that six songs barely make a cohesive story. But the music was of such a high quality, it gave the band its first chart entry – and, as I said before, there are Gentle Giant aficionados who rate this as their favourite album. Any hopes, however, that this would also herald a more stable line-up were dashed when drummer Mortimore broke his arm and leg and cracked his pelvis in a motorcycle accident. A replacement had to be found for an impending tour, so Ray contacted Grease Band drummer John 'Pugwash' Weathers, who had supported Simon Dupree and the Big Sound when he was in Eyes of Blue.

Mortimore recalled to *Prog* magazine in 2017: 'I went to see them. I was in a wheelchair. They were keen to keep working, keep as tight as they could. Phil called me up and said, "Malcolm, I'm sorry to say this, you're fitting in really well, but John's got to stay". I said, "Alright, that's it" – they were off to America and that was that'.

Weathers had an immediate impact on the band's sound – they were heavier and more rhythmic with him in the engine room. He also introduced Minnear to James Brown's 'Sex Machine', inspiring him to write more rhythmic pieces. Minnear said in the same article: 'John's solid approach changed the way we sounded as a band and the way we wrote. We could be more rhythmically adventurous with such a strong foundation. We were settling into our identity as a band and what characteristics were unique to us'.

By the time GG started recording again in July 1972, they were a tight musical unit, having toured with Black Sabbath, Yes and Jethro Tull, and even supported a film of Jimi Hendrix. This is reflected in the second album they released in 1972 – the music is heavier, more confident and appears to be simpler. Certainly, the tracks are all shorter than most of the cuts on *Three Friends*, with only the closer, 'River', breaking the five-minute mark.

Once again, this was intended to be a concept album, this time based on the characters in the band and the roadies. As the writing process went on, the concept was dropped in favour of simply writing good songs that rocked a bit more than usual, with lyrics that fitted perfectly. Green told *Prog* magazine:

I'd heard some of Yes and Genesis – they were too far out for me. We all liked something a bit more real that you could get your teeth into – we were a bit more of a working-class prog band than the others. Even though we had highfalutin concepts – RD Laing, Camus and Rabelais – they made more real-life sense to me. We were a bit more in the dirt.

Mmm, well, maybe. Opening track, 'The Advent of Panurge', is not necessarily what you would call 'in the dirt'. The lyrics refer to one of the chapters by the aforementioned Francois Rabelais, whose most famous work is a series of books known as *Gargantua And Pantagruel*, written between 1532 and 1548. Ostensibly comic fantasies involving jolly giants having humorous, absurd adventures, they were also satirical comments on Roman Catholic society that turned accepted norms on their heads to make philosophical points. Frequently vulgar and licentious, they were condemned by both secular and religious authorities.

Gentle Giant had borrowed from Rabelais for an earlier track on the second album, 'Pantagruel's Nativity'. For 'The Advent of Panurge', they turned to the ninth chapter, entitled 'How Pantagruel Found Panurge, Whom He Loved All His Life'. Pantagruel says: 'Do you see that man coming along the road from the Charenton bridge? On my faith, he is only poor in fortune. His physiognomy tells me for certain that he comes of some rich and noble stock'. This inspires the opening lines of the song, 'There coming over Charenton Bridge/Look do you see the man who is poor but rich'.

The song opens with the meeting, sung by Minnear and accompanied only by bass and guitar lines. In fact, nearly a minute elapses before new drummer Weathers makes his appearance. When he does, it's to provide some heavy rhythmic support to an instrumental section led by piano, with Green playing repetitive lead figures over the top. There are sporadic blasts of brass played by Phil and Derek on saxes, trumpet and mellophone, an instrument rather like a bugle. In the middle of the song are some indistinct words that sound like a foreign tongue – it's hard to make them out, so it is difficult to suggest what language they are in. What we do know is they are not French, because, in the original story, Panurge speaks to Pantagruel in every language other than the one he understands.

Packed into this track are all the musical motifs that make Gentle Giant unique – the contrast between loud and soft, the almost baroque tinkling of the verses crashing up against rocking, swinging sections, the apparent lack of any structure, the dense, complicated lyrics that became totally indecipherable, and the final, sudden ending on the word 'hell'. 'The Advent of Panurge' was both a band and fan favourite that stayed in the repertoire right up to the end.

Second track, 'Raconteur Troubadour', also belies Green's claim the band were more 'in the dirt' – it's an attempt to create a modern version of a mediaeval minstrel, with simple, repetitive melody lines and lyrics that open with 'Gather round the village square/Come good people both wretched and fair/See the troubadour play on the drum/Hear my songs on the lute that I strum'. However, lead vocalist Phil is accompanied by thrumming bass violin and cello rather than lute. And I suspect very few troubadours sang songs in alternate bars of 5/4 and 6/4.

This being Gentle Giant, the song jumps into a fast instrumental section led by swift keyboard arpeggios as violin plays the verse melody over the top. Then there's a stately string section that could almost be the theme to a Downton Abbey-style period TV drama, followed by a trumpet fanfare before we go back to the verse melody. Weathers gets little to do here with his drumkit beyond providing bass drum thumps and some jazzy stuff on the cymbals during the fast section.

'A Cry For Everyone' opens like a more straightforward rock song, with fuzzed-up power chords from Green and a fairly 4/4, foot-to-the-floor rhythm. Now this is a bit dirty – being Gentle Giant, it stops and starts practically all the way through, with organ and piano flourishes that mess with the tempo and your head. The subject matter is pretty downbeat, being inspired by the works of French philosopher/author Albert Camus, who believed human life was essentially worthless. 'If I could cry, I'd cry for everyone./Doubts, no doubt, is all I know./There is no fate, there's no luck, what does that show', sings Derek. It shows you need to read some more cheerful books, Del.

Track four, 'Knots', is also inspired by literature; in this case, the work of Scottish psychiatrist RD Laing, who wrote extensively on mental illness and was opposed to the use of electroconvulsive therapy in the treatment of schizophrenia – indeed, he wasn't sure the condition actually existed. He seems to have been a fan of *The Ashley Book of Knots*, written in 1944 by American sailor Clifford Ashley, and, well, all about knots, really. This may have inspired Laing to look at the 'knots' in our lives – the intricacies of human relationships – described in dense, impenetrable dialogue scenarios in his 1970 book, *Knots*.

So the song title works on a number of levels; it refers to the knotty subject of relationships, but also the tangled way Laing wrote. To understand the song, you have to unravel its meaning. Musically, this is an example of Gentle Giant's ability to create interlocking four-piece vocal harmonies – the band was blessed with four good singers with impeccable timing and pitch.

'Knots' (the song) opens as a sort of chant, with the seemingly random nature of the vocals echoed by equally random tinkling and parping from xylophone, violin and sax. The full band come in for a jig-like rhythm in the middle before a return to a xylophone and piano duet, with dramatic, King Crimson-like interruptions, ending with repetitive chanting, somewhat reminiscent of Carl Orff's Carmina Burana. Knotty in both lyrical and musical content, the song became a Gentle Giant classic and a live favourite.

Side two of the original vinyl opened with the sound of laughter and a spinning coin (that would inspire Emerson, Lake & Palmer to start their *Trilogy* album with a heartbeat) before launching into 'The Boys in the Band' – perhaps a hangover from the original concept. It's an instrumental, opening in Frank Zappa style with a tumble of notes led by saxophone and organ, before entering a more straightforward 4/4 section that gives Green a chance to shine on guitar over chunky bass. Being Gentle Giant, the track moves through various jazzy sections in which time signatures are virtually thrown to the wind before fading out on the opening theme.

'Dog's Life' is another track that stemmed from the original plan to write musical pieces about the band. In this case, the lyrics compare a faithful roadie to an equally loyal but somewhat broken-down old canine! It's the shortest and sparsest track on the album, combining the sounds of a mediaeval reed organ and strings under comedic verses about the old dog shuffling down the street.

The gentler mood continues with 'Think of Me With Kindness', a mostly piano-based ballad and relatively simple (for Gentle Giant, anyway). Sung plaintively and appealingly by Kerry, it contains some beautiful melodic lines and a grand ending with trumpet and organ accompaniment. The title speaks for itself: 'fare thee well, you that was once dear to me', sings Minnear. A bitter-sweet song about parting.

The album ends with 'River', another multi-sectioned song with solid drumming, urgent violin riffs, plenty of stops and starts, a somewhat atonal melody and lots of organ flourishes. It's the longest track on the album and packs more into its 5:55 than most bands do in their careers! Various electronic devices are used to create whooshes and juddering sound effects in an attempt to create mysterious atmospheres; Weathers' commanding drumming holds everything together and Green gets a guitar solo at the end.

Phil's wife, Roberta, allegedly named the album – there are eight (Octo) opuses (although another plural for opus is opera, which is even more musical). On release, it was hailed as the band's best album so far and it has stood the test of time well, listed at 65 in *Prog* magazine's 100 Greatest Prog Albums of All Time. Not bad for a band that really shied away from commercial success in its early days. As Derek later said in a 2014 interview with *Hit Channel*:

We were just Gentle Giant and we were just a band of musicians who were pushing ourselves to become better musicians for each other, for the band and for our compositions, and ultimately to become a band of fairly good musicians who can play music for fans who would enjoy music that we put together. So, ultimately it was just an incarnation of who we were individually as musicians and hopefully, the fans would come along and would enjoy what we had put together. This was the only reason for existence. We didn't do it for fame, money or any other experience rather than just to make really enjoyable music together.

Aphrodite's Child – *666*

Personnel:
Vangelis Papathanassiou (Evangelos Odysseas Papathanassiou): keyboards, organ, piano, vibraphone, bass, flute, percussion, backing vocals
Demis Roussos (Artemios Ventouris-Roussos): lead vocal, bass, guitar, trumpet, backing vocals
Loukas Sideras: drums, lead vocals on "The Beast", "Break", backing vocals
Silver Koulouris (Anargyros Koulouris): guitar, percussion
Recorded 1970-1971 at Studio Europa Sonar, Paris, France
Produced by Vangelis Papathanassiou.
Production assistance by Giorgio Gomelsky
Engineered by Roger Roche and Jean-Claude Conan
Label: Vertigo
Release date: June 1972
Truncated version released in Brazil as *Break*
Chart places: Italy: 23
Tracks: 'The System', 'Babylon', 'Loud, Loud, Loud', 'The Four Horsemen', 'The Lamb', 'The Seventh Seal', 'Aegian Sea', 'Seven Bowls', 'The Wakening Beast', 'Lament', 'The Marching Beast', 'The Battle of the Locusts', 'Do it', 'Tribulation', 'The Beast', 'Ofis', 'Seven Trumpets', 'Altamont', 'The Wedding of the Lamb', 'The Capture of the Beast', ' "∞" (Infinity)', 'Hic Et Nunc', 'All the Seats Were Occupied', 'Break'
All tracks composed by Vangelis Papathanassiou and Costas Ferris.

The story so far...

Greek-born keyboard player Evangelos Odysseas Papathanassiou – better known as Vangelis – developed an interest in music at the tender age of four and later started pop group The Forminx in 1963 with school pals. After the band broke up in 1966, he composed music for Greek films before meeting singer and bassist Artemios Ventouris-Roussos – born in Egypt to Greek parents and better known as Demis Roussos – two years later. Roussos also studied music at an early age and played in Greek bands, including The Idols. The pair got together with drummer Loukas Sideras, from Athens, and guitarist Anargyros 'Silver' Koulouris, from Piraeus, to form a band. Originally called Vangelis and His Orchestra, the quartet attempted to relocate to London but ended up in Paris, renaming themselves Aphrodite's Child after a track on an album by label mate Dick Campbell. Their first US-only single flopped but follow-up 'Rain and Tears' was a huge international hit. Their first album, *End of the World*, failed to chart but their second LP, *It's Five O'Clock*, reached number one in France and number six in Italy. Subsequent singles 'I Want to Live', 'It's Five O'Clock' and 'Spring, Summer, Winter, Fall' kept the band in the charts in some parts of Europe. Vangelis scored more films, while Roussos was being groomed for a solo career. But there was one more Aphrodite's Child album to come.

The album

The Four Horsemen of the Apocalypse. The Fall of Babylon. The big, bad, wicked Beast. A circus staged by God. The final battle between Good and Evil. And real orgasms.

No, not a night trawling through the darkest recesses of social media but a disturbing double album released in 1972 to almost total indifference but now revered as a cult classic. And it came from a short-lived Greek band that included a composer best known for his synth-based film soundtracks and a portly, kaftan-wearing housewives' favourite who warbled songs in a voice apparently high on helium.

Aphrodite's Child were best known, if they were known at all, for their 1968 single, 'Rain And Tears', which added new lyrics to seventeenth-century German composer Johann Paschebel's Canon in D Major and hit number one all over the place (although only peaked at number 29 in the UK). Yes, their sound was unusual, thanks to Roussos's high-pitched, operatic vocals and Vangelis's gloomy soundscape approach to his music. Their second album, in particular, covers a variety of styles, from the nod to Procol Harum in 'It's Five O'Clock', the pub blues of 'Wake Up', the country folk of 'Take Your Time' and the greasy funk of 'Funky Mary'.

But no one, particularly the record company, expected the band to record a double album based on the *Book of Revelation*, the final book in the Christian Bible and traditionally ascribed to John of Patmos, who was exiled to the Greek island of the same name during the reign of the Roman emperor Domitian. In fact, so shocked were Mercury Records – particularly by the five minutes of orgasmic noises on '∞' – they refused to release it. By the time it came out on Mercury's more experimental Vertigo label, Aphrodite's Child had broken up and gone their separate ways.

The story of *666* starts, as many stories do, with a meeting – on this occasion, between Vangelis and film director Costas Ferris, who, in 1966, wanted to make a movie about The Forminx. The film was never completed after original director Theo Angelopolous spent five days just shooting the band members' legs as they walked around Thessaloniki. A few years later, Ferris asked Vangelis to score a movie he had co-written called Aquarius – the musician turned it down. But, says Ferris in an interview for *vangelislyrics.com*:

Two days later, he called me to tell me that he loved the script and he wanted, from me, a good idea for a concept album by Aphrodite's Child. He knew already that the group was about to split and the one and only 'star' who could make a solo career was Demis. So he wanted to make a final record which could put in value his composing talent. I came back two more days later, with two concepts: The Jesus Christ passion, seen through the eyes of the Sixties, with Jesus seen as a Great Star being sacrificed; and Saint John's 'Revelation' (The Apocalypse as we call it in Greek). That subject, too, had to be seen through the culture of the Sixties.

61

Vangelis opted for the latter, so Ferris wrote a concept story inspired by the Book of Revelation and heavily influenced by The Beatles' *Sgt Pepper's Lonely Hearts Club Band*. It depicted a circus performance, based on the Apocalypse, taking place in a tent. But outside, God himself is staging the real Apocalypse as foretold in the *Book of Revelation*, the end of the world and all that. It culminates in a great battle between Good and Evil and a splendid time is guaranteed for all.

From Ferris's own description of his work, it seems as if he may have intended to create some sort of stage show or performance – he talks about his concept as a 'book', in the same way a musical has a 'book' with the script and the stage directions. He also claimed to have played a part in other concept albums such as The Who's *Tommy* – a close friend was Kit Lambert, then manager of The Who.

The album was composed without any input from the rest of the band, which had virtually ceased to exist by this time, so all the tracks are credited to Vangelis and Ferris, even the instrumentals. When Roussos, Sideras and Koulouris were summoned to the Paris recording studio, they weren't happy with the concept at all. They wanted to continue with the psychedelic pop that had brought them a fair amount of success, clashing with Vangelis, who found the commercial approach 'boring'. Tensions were so high that the quartet refused to talk to each other after every take, communicating only through engineer Roche.

The band took three months to record the album, pulling in additional musicians where necessary, including Greek actress and singer Irene Papas, who died aged 93 just a few days before this sentence was written. It was her performance on '∞ (Infinity)' that caused Mercury Records to baulk at releasing the album – she was required to chant, 'I am, I am to come, I was' while, apparently, experiencing an orgasm. According to Siduras, the accommodating Ms Papas may not have been acting. He said: 'Was she happy to do it? Very, very much! It was real, you know? She was alone in her own cabin and no one was allowed to look at her. It was all dark in the room and that's how she did it. It wasn't a theatrical thing; it was a real orgasm'.

Also on hand to help was Giorgio Gomelsky, famous for managing and producing bands such as The Rolling Stones, The Yardbirds, Magma and Gong, who contrived to 'pass by' the studio because he admired the band so much. He became a kind of acting producer, selecting narrators for the spoken word sections and generally providing uncredited assistance.

The result is an unpredictable, dishevelled, disturbing and, sometimes, overwhelming album. The mixture of rock, jazz, musique concrete and electronic experimentation is Zappa-esque in its sonic variety, and, like Zappa's work, is not without a sense of humour. For example, the album sleeve announced that it was 'recorded under the influence of SAHLEP'. This led some, including the record label, to believe it was extolling the virtues of drug-taking or that Sahlep was some kind of Greek demon. In fact, it is a sort of calming herbal tea.

It opens with a statement inspired by the writings of American political activist Albert 'Abbie' Hoffman, whose manifesto was outlined in a 1967 pamphlet, 'Fuck the System'. On 666, it's a paradoxical chant – 'We've got the system to fuck the system' – that builds in intensity over just 23 seconds before segueing into the Byrds-like, jangling guitar intro to the insanely catchy 'Babylon'. Roussos sings that Babylon has fallen (as indeed it did in 539 BCE when it was conquered by the Achaemenid empire) accompanied by the sound of cheering crowds. The rather lumpen drums are actually played by Vangelis, not Sideras, and there are blasts of brass from Roussos and trombonist Michel Ripoche.

Simple piano chords introduce narration by a child called Daniel Koplowitz, apparently the son of a diplomat, whose spoken words are interspersed with chants of 'loud, loud, loud' by a chorus of children. That leads directly into 'The Four Horsemen', which alternates gentle verses with a pounding, catchy chorus, followed by a long, spirited guitar solo by Koulouris over a repetitive sequence of the major chords: E, D, C, D, C, D and E.

The song crossfades into the first instrumental on the album, a kind of fast jazz and Middle Eastern folk hybrid, the melody played on what sounds like a traditional Greek reed instrument but is probably a keyboard patch, accompanied by wordless chanting and punctuated with swift, syncopated keyboard flourishes. The final track on side one, 'The Seventh Seal', is a gentle keyboard and string melody with narration by John Forst that paraphrases chapter six of the *Book of Revelation*, in which a very busy lamb opens many seals.

Another instrumental, the dreamy 'Aegian Sea' (as spelt on the album), opens side two, with Koulouris providing guitar solos over Vangelis's keyboard washes and wordless vocals, and Forst returns to reprise some of his narration from the preceding track. 'Seven Bowls' offers more chanting as a softly-spoken chorus narrates the story of the set of plagues mentioned in Revelation 16 over apparently random, untuned percussion effects. That leads imperceptibly into 'The Wakening Beast', an eerie instrumental with tinkling wind chimes.

'Lament' has Roussos singing, 'alas for the human race', over the drone of a single note played on vibraphone and very bassy keyboard, sounding like a distant Muslim call to prayer. Then there's another instrumental, 'The Marching Beast', played mostly on piano with added saxophone and bass, while 'The Battle of the Locusts' is a brief, 56-second rock instrumental with wailing guitar over two alternating chords. 'Do It' is another guitar improvisation with rapid drumming and the title repeated at odd intervals – a reference to a 1970 book by another US political activist, Jerry Rubin. Both Rubin and Hoffman, mentioned above, were members of the so-called Chicago Eight, who were accused of incitement to riot at the 1968 Democratic National Convention.

There's yet another short instrumental, the sax-led, jazz-inspired 'Tribulation' before we reach a proper song, the bouncy 'The Beast', which is little more than a few lines sung over two alternating chords, ending in a guitar instrumental. It's lifted by the occasional insertion of a 6/4 bar into what is mostly a straightforward 4/4 rock song, and the addition of a few random words and phrases – during recording, Vangelis gave instructions to the other band members and some of his commands were deemed rhythmically interesting enough to be peppered throughout the song. Finally, side two ends with the shortest track on the album, just sixteen seconds of Greek painter Yiannis Tsarouhis, saying a line from the Greek play *Karagiozis, Alexander the Great and the Cursed Serpent*, the best-known example of the centuries-old shadow theatre tradition.

So far, so bitty – we've had sixteen tracks spread across two sides of the original vinyl, half of them less than two minutes in length. That changes on the next two sides – quite radically in the case of the penultimate track on the album – but we kick off with yet another short one. In 'Seven Trumpets', Forst paraphrases Revelation 8-11, in which seven trumpets herald apocalyptic events. This is the moment when the circus tent comes down and the apocalyptic entertainment of the show collides with the real Apocalypse happening in the real world.

We segue into the piano-led pounding of 'Altamont', accompanied by jazzy horns and Roussos's wordless scatting. Altamont was, of course, the infamous free concert in December 1969 that degenerated into deadly violence and pretty much signalled the end of the 'peace and love' of the late Sixties. There's narration over the music that references the bowls and serpents and trumpets but also proclaims, 'We are the people, the rolling people'. Could this be a reference to The Rolling Stones, who headlined Altamont and were performing when Meredith Hunter was stabbed to death by a Hell's Angel?

'Altamont' crossfades into 'The Wedding of the Lamb', a whirling instrumental led by flute-like keyboards with rhythmic drumming that certainly suggests a wild dance at a satanic wedding. A voice announces the track's title, there is a brief drum solo, and the voice returns to say: 'And now, the capture of the beast'. For that is indeed the title of the next track, basically a drum solo by Sideras overlaid by keyboard sounds and drones.

We then come to the most controversial track on the album, '∞', which is also known as 'Infinity'. As stated above, it features Irene Papas apparently orgasming over random percussion. It was originally 39 minutes long, which must have exhausted Ms Papas, and was supposed to portray the pain of childbirth and the joy of sexual intercourse. Vangelis then decided to add metallic percussion noises and the whole thing was improvised in the studio. Edited down for release, it was still too much for Mercury Records, who demanded it be cut. Vangelis refused, leading to the album being stuck in the vaults for a year, but he did eventually reduce it to its final 5:15 length.

The crowd noises from 'Babylon' return for 'Hic Et Nunc', an upbeat pop

Right: Jethro Tull in 1972: From left to right, Barriemore Barlow, Ian Anderson, John Evan, Martin Barre and Jeffrey Hammond. (*Gijsbert Hanekroot/ Redferns*)

Left: Peter Gabriel in full flight during 'Watcher Of The Skies'. (*Getty Images*)

Above: Yes in the studio, with (left to right), Chris Squire, Steve Howe, Jon Anderson and Rick Wakeman. (*Getty Images*)

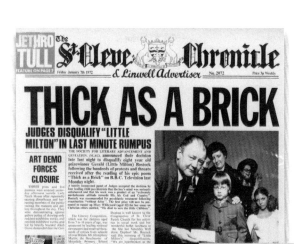

Left: The cover of *Thick As A Brick* – designed to look like a broadsheet local newspaper – took longer to create than the music! (*Chrysalis Records*)

Right: Peter Gabriel was inspired by the cover of *Foxtrot* to wear a fox head and his wife's red dress on stage. (*Charisma Records*)

Left: *Close To The Edge* had a gatefold sleeve designed by Roger Dean, although the front cover was uncharacteristically restrained. (*Atlantic Records*)

Right: Salvador Dali was too expensive, so design company Hipgnosis came up with the cover of Emerson, Lake & Palmer's album *Trilogy*. (*Island Records*)

Left: Another Hipgnosis design, this time for Pink Floyd's *Obscured By Clouds*. The cover is a completely distorted still from the film *La Vallee*. (*Harvest Records*)

Right: The simple, stark cover of *666* is in complete contrast to the chaotic nature of the music. (*Vertigo Records*)

Left: Keith Emerson, Carl Palmer and Greg Lake were all perfectionists with massive egos. (*Island Records*)

Right: David Gilmour takes centre stage as Pink Floyd perform in Amsterdam in 1972. (*Gijsbert Hanekroot/ Redferns*)

Left: Gentle Giant after the departure of Phil Shulman. Left to right, they were Gary Green, Kerry Minnear, John Weathers, Derek Schulman and Ray Schulman. (*Vertigo Records*)

Right: Aphrodite's Child had broken up by the time their prog classic *666* was released in 1972. (*Vertigo Records*)

Left: PFM released two albums in 1972 that are widely seen as prog rock classics. (*Numero Uno*)

Right: The inimitable Robert Wyatt was Matching Mole's drummer, songwriter and driving force until a fall left him in a wheelchair for the rest of his life. (*CBS Records*)

Left: Gentle Giant's *Three Friends* was their first album to chart in the US. (*Vertigo Records*)

Right: Roger Dean provided the artwork for *Octopus*, which set the template for many of the subsequent Gentle Giant albums. (*Vertigo Records*)

Left: Matching Mole's name was based on the French translation of Soft Machine, Robert Wyatt's previous band. (*CBS Records*)

Right: PFM's debut album, *Storia Di Un Minuto,* topped the Italian album charts. (*Numero Uno*)

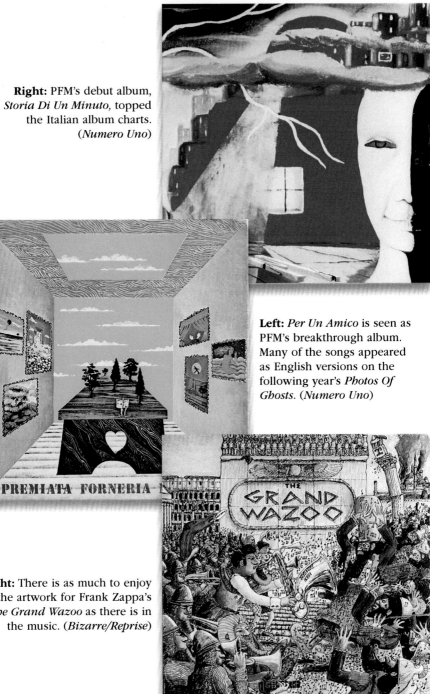

Left: *Per Un Amico* is seen as PFM's breakthrough album. Many of the songs appeared as English versions on the following year's *Photos Of Ghosts.* (*Numero Uno*)

Right: There is as much to enjoy in the artwork for Frank Zappa's *The Grand Wazoo* as there is in the music. (*Bizarre/Reprise*)

Left: Swedish musician Bo Hansson pictured in the studio recording *Lord Of The Rings.* (*Ninni Warme*)

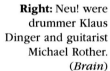

Right: Neu! were drummer Klaus Dinger and guitarist Michael Rother. (*Brain*)

Left: The Strawbs were originally The Strawberry Hill Boys – but by 1972 they had left their folk roots far behind. (*A&M Records*)

Right: Focus in 1972. From left to right, Jan Akkerman, Bert Ruiter, Thijs van Leer and Pierre van der Linden. (*Imperial Records*)

Left: Santana's big breakthrough was at Woodstock – but by 1972 the band was falling apart. (*Alamy*)

Right: Curved Air in 1972: Francis Monkman, left, Florian Pilkington-Miksa, Mike Wedgewood, Sonja Kristina and Darryl Way. (*Curved Air*)

Left: The pop-art cover of Neu!'s debut album, recognised as a 'landmark of German experimental rock'. (*Brain*)

Right: The cover of The Strawbs' *Grave New World* used a William Blake painting. (*A&M Records*)

Left: *Focus 3* contained the band's hit single 'Sylvia'. (*Imperial Records*)

Right: Santana's record company thought *Caravanserai* was commercial suicide. (*Columbia Records*)

Left: Curved Air broke up (for the first time) soon after the release of *Phantasmagoria*. (*Warner Records*)

Right: Can's third album *Ege Bamyasi* depicted a can of Aegean okra. (*United Artists Records*)

Above: The members of Banco del Mutuo Soccorso in a light-hearted studio shot. (*Ricordi*)

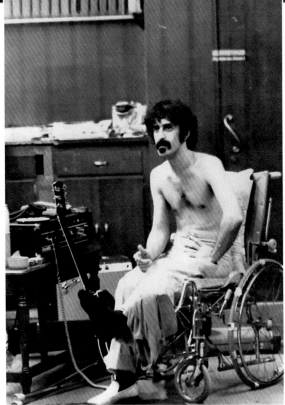

Right: Frank Zappa in a wheelchair after being pushed off stage at London's Rainbow Theatre. (*Universal Music Group*)

Above: Four of the five members of Can's 1972 line-up. From left to right, they are Jaki Liebezeit, Holger Czukay, Irmin Schmidt and Michael Karoli. (*Faber & Faber*)

Below: Uriah Heep overcame critical condescension to make arguably their best and most proggy album in 1972. (*Fin Costello/Getty Images*)

Left: Banco del Mutuo Soccorso's self-titled debut had a cover cut in the shape of a terracotta piggy bank. (*Ricordi*)

Right: Their second album *Darwin!* is regarded as a classic of 1970s progressive rock. (*Ricordi*)

Left: Uriah Heep's *Demons and Wizards* had a cover designed by the go-to man for album artwork, Roger Dean. (*Bronze/Island*)

Right: Bo Hansson initially released *Saga Om Ringen* in 1970. It became a huge hit in Sweden. (*Silence Records*)

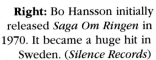

Left: Two years later, Bo's epic was released in the rest of the world – but its title changed to *Music inspired by The Lord Of The Rings* after complaints from the Tolkien family. (*Charisma*)

Right: Caravan's *Waterloo Lily* went down a more jazzy route after the departure of keyboard player David Sinclair. *(Deram)*

Left: Nektar's second album *A Tab In The Ocean* is regarded by fans as their best. (*Bellaphon Records*)

Right: Family began as a progressive rock band but gradually became more mainstream – despite John Wetton appearing on their sixth studio album *Bandstand*. (*Reprise*)

Left: *Prologue* was the third studio album by a band called Renaissance but is regarded as the first with a nearly all-new line-up. (*Sovereign*)

song featuring phased piano and tenor sax. The title is Latin for 'here and now', which is what the crowd sings in the chorus. There are traces of the band Traffic in the melody lines and Roussos's vocals, and the whole thing fades out on a guitar solo to end side three.

Side four contains just two songs, one of which is the nineteen-minute monster instrumental, 'All the Seats Were Occupied', in which elements of at least a dozen of the preceding tracks make an appearance. It starts as a slow-building, contemplative raga-like drone before slashing guitar chords and powerful drums pick up the pace, with a simple, repetitive keyboard melody playing over the top. The keyboard starts improvising, snippets of previous tracks add to the cacophony, a piano pounds tunelessly before taking over with stabbing chords and a guitar adds plucked notes in an eastern scale. The drumming gets louder and there are congas from guest musician Harris Halkitis (who also provides bass and tenor sax on the sessions).

At about the nine-minute mark, the instruments fade away and we are left with wordless harmony chanting, like monks calling to their god on a Himalayan hillside. Then electric guitar notes return, back come the drums and bass, and off we go for another instrumental gallop, with snippets of Irene Papas allegedly pleasuring herself in the studio. By the way, all this is in the single chord of D minor, with no sign that it's ever going to change.

A bass riff takes over in a tricky-dicky time signature, there's lead guitar over the top, staying within those eastern scales, and the drums drive the whole thing onwards. Everything stops suddenly for the title to be announced – it came from a BBC language teaching record – before ending in a cacophony of sound.

Despite the fact that there are no lyrics, no chord changes and little in the way of any discernible melodies, the track goes surprisingly quickly and hangs together well as a mixture of group improvisation and musique concrete. Three cheers and a tiger must go to Loukas Sideras, whose muscular, unstoppable drumming keeps everything together. As the final clash between Good and Evil, it's perhaps not quite as awe-inspiring as it could have been but I like the way it rounds up the album by reprising previous tracks.

There is one final song on 666, one that doesn't really fit the story, although it serves as a farewell from the band as well as the human race. 'Break' is a pretty piano-based ballad sung by Sideras, with Vangelis adding nonsense scat vocals in a jazzy, call-and-response way. It finishes with the word 'Do It', reprised from the earlier track. Released as a single, with 'Babylon' on the B-side, it failed to 'Break' into the charts (except in Holland) or do anything to promote the album.

When Mercury Records refused to release 666, the band organised a protest party at the recording studio. One of the guests, Salvador Dali, heard the album, loved it and came up with plans for a 'happening' in Barcelona to launch it. Suggested events included declaring martial law for the day, blowing up live swans with dynamite and bombing La Sagrada Familia, Antoni Gaudi's still unfinished art nouveau church, with elephants, hippopotami, whales and archbishops carrying umbrellas. Needless to say, the launch did not take place.

The album was finally released in June 1972, more than a year after it had been completed, sporting a striking red cover with the title in white out of black like a car number plate. Additional wording meant the full title could arguably be *Anyone Who Has Intelligence May Interpret the Number of the Beast. It is a Man's Number. This Number is 666 (The Apocalypse of John, 13/18)*. The band had split by then, with Vangelis concentrating on his soundtrack career. Roussos, Sideras and Koulouris briefly reformed to tour the album before they, too, went their separate ways.

666 pretty much passed under the radar of contemporary critics but has since been judged 'an amazingly bombastic concept album' by *Allmusic*, containing 'great dollops of proggy weirdness, wildly experimental forms, eerie vocal chants' (*Classic Rock*), and 'a double-disc marathon of visionary Greco-prog madness' (*Mojo*). It sufficiently impressed Jon Anderson to invite Vangelis to join Yes, and the duo had a short but successful stint together that resulted in the hit singles 'I'll Find My Way Home', 'State of Independence' and 'I Hear You Now'. Meanwhile, Roussos warbled his way into the charts with inoffensive little ditties such as 'Forever and Ever', which hit number one in several countries, including the UK.

It's almost impossible to believe that the 'Chariots of Fire' composer and the kaftanned crooner were once part of a group that created one of prog's darkest and most disturbing concept albums. But here it is, as progressive an album as you will ever hear and still overpowering and magnificent 50 years later.

Premiata Forneria Marconi – *Storia Di Un Minuto* & *Per Un Amico*

Personnel:
Franz Di Cioccio: drums, Moog, gadgets, backing vocals
Franco Mussida: guitars, mandocello, lead vocals, backing vocals
Mauro Pagani: flute, piccolo, violin, backing vocals
Giorgio Piazza: bass, backing vocals
Flavio Premoli: keyboards, lead and backing vocals
Storia Di Un Minuto recorded 1971 at Fonorama Studios, Milan
Produced by Claudio Fabi and PFM
Engineered by Gaetano Ria
Label: Numero Uno
Release date: Italy in January 1972. Later releases on RCA and BMG.
Chart places: Italy: 1
Tracks: 'Introduzione' (Mussida), 'Impressioni di settembre' (Mussida, Mogol, Pagani), 'E festa', 'Dove...quando...(parte 1)', 'Dove...quando...(parte 2), 'La carrozza di Hans', 'Grazie davvero'
All tracks written by Mussida and Pagani except as noted.
Per Un Amico recorded in 1972 at Fonorama Studios, Milan
Produced by Premiata Forneria Marconi in collaboration with Claudio Fabi
Engineered by Gaetano Ria
Label: Numero Uno
Release date: Italy in November 1972. Later releases on RCA.
Chart places: did not chart
Tracks: 'Appena Un Po'', 'Generale' (Mussida, Premoli), 'Per Un Amico', 'Il Banchetto', 'Geranio'
All tracks written by Mussida, Pagani and Premoli except as noted.

The story so far...

In 1964, Di Cioccio and Mussida, both from Milan, were members of beat group The Black Devils, who soon changed their name to I Quelli and had a few hit singles, interrupted by Mussida leaving to do national service in the Italian navy. In 1966, bassist Piazza, from Genova, joined, followed by Varese-born Premoli in 1967, from the short-lived group I Cuccioli. Mussida returned and the quartet released a 1969 album that included covers of Deep Purple's hit 'Hush' and 'The Thoughts of Emerlist Davjack' from the debut by The Nice. They also worked as in-demand session musicians. Joined by Pagani, from Chiari, Lombardy, they signed to Numero Uno – later sold to RCA – and took the name Premiata Forneria Marconi.

The album

The Italians love progressive rock, perhaps even more so than the British. At the risk of making generalised comments about racial characteristics, the music seems to match the stereotypical idea of the flamboyant, demonstrative, unrestrained Italians. After all, this is the country that invented opera, surely classical music's most dramatic and theatrical offspring – the word means 'work' in Italian, and the earliest opera, Dafne, was composed in 1597 by Roman musician Jacopi Peri. The Italians also appreciate skill and flair, which prog has in abundance, so it is no surprise that they embraced it in the early 1970s, becoming the first country to send a Genesis album to the top of the charts when the UK was shrugging its shoulders with indifference.

The country was quick to produce its own homegrown prog bands and chief of these were Premiata Forneria Marconi. What a powerful name, eh? Unfortunately, it translates as 'Award-winning Marconi Bakery' – Forneria Marconi was the name of a shop, and they added the 'Premiata' to make it sound a bit more impressive as if the band were some kind of musical workshop. The record label complained that the name was too long, but the band reasoned this would make them memorable. In the event, King Crimson lyricist Pete Sinfield encouraged them to refer to themselves as PFM, which was much less of a mouthful. But they started a trend in long, unwieldy Italian band names – would Banco Del Mutuo Soccorso have existed without them?

They came at a time when British progressive rock bands were becoming hugely popular in Italy – not only Genesis but Procol Harum and Yes were welcomed with open arms. PFM's moment came when they were booked as 'guest stars' for the opening night in Bologna of Deep Purple's Italian tour. Kicking off with a cover of Crimson's '21st Century Schizoid Man' (in total darkness because nobody had put the lights on), their performance was such a success, they became popular festival artists. For one such event, the Viareggio Festival dedicated to new trends in music, bands were challenged to perform an unpublished song in competition – it was won by PFM with Mussida's composition, 'La carroza di Hans' (translated as 'Hans' Coach'). It was released as a single, backed with 'Impressione di Settembre' ('September Feelings'), hitting number nine in the Italian singles chart. An album was the next inevitable step.

But first, they needed a few more instruments to fill out their sound. They had heard Emerson, Lake & Palmer's 'Lucky Man' and loved what Keith Emerson could do with his Moog synthesiser. But a Moog was still hellishly expensive and beyond the reach of many bands – PFM certainly didn't have the money to buy one. But what they did have, it seems, was a good line in persuasive patter – they convinced an Italian stockist to *give* them a Moog, promising him he would sell ten of them once the band started using it on stage.

They also envied King Crimson's Mellotron, used to such great effect on the band's explosive debut *In the Court of the Crimson King*, but had never seen one in the flesh, so to speak, before attending a gig by Scottish prog band Beggars Opera. There they saw the strange instrument in action on stage and immediately bought it (along with employing the only person from the

Beggars Opera crew who knew how to use it). Di Cioccio said on the band's website *pfmpfm.it*:

The Mellotron was a very complicated instrument. It was not easy to move daily, as it was like a recorder with many tapes supported by springs. Its keys could move every tape, but unfortunately, the tapes could tangle very easily every time the Mellotron was moved. It had to be handled with care and after every movement, it had to be set up; otherwise, it sounded like an angry marine cow! Every time we had to move the Mellotron, it was a problem; it had to be treated like a relic! Anyway, it looked really extraordinary because it was an enormous woody catafalque! People could not help looking at it ... we discovered many surprises recorded on the tapes: the famous guitar scale from the Beatles' 'Bungalow Bill' on the first key, a hit from The Moody Blues on the second one. In 'La Carrozza di Hans', we used some violin chords and the final effect was really unbelievable.

Armed with a Moog, Mellotron and a hit single, PFM booked into Fonorama Studios in Milan, owned by well-known composer and record producer Carlo Alberto Rossi, to record their debut album. Most of it was done live as a band with minimal overdubs because they wanted to sound immediate and energetic. The result is an album that certainly wears its influences on its sleeve – the symphonic sounds of Yes, the jazzy flute of Jethro Tull, the Mellotron drama of King Crimson, the Moog pyrotechnics of ELP and the stylistic leaps of Gentle Giant. But there was enough of PFM's personality in there – along with their spine-tingling use of dynamics and an ear for exquisite melodies – to put their own stamp on the music and create something new and exciting.

After a short introduction that seeps gently out of the speakers before crashing into a crunchy guitar riff, we segue into the B-side of the hit single, which pretty much sets the template for the PFM sound – a dreamy, acoustic-led introduction under Mussida's contemplative vocals, peppered with Pagani's flute stylings, that builds into a lengthy Moog and guitar riff acting as an instrumental chorus, set on a sea of warm Mellotron strings. Composed mostly by Di Cioccio in his parents' living room, it was the song that persuaded the band to get some better instruments, because the refrain needed more body than they could achieve with guitars and flute. The album version is about a minute longer than the single release – the band added a bit more to the quiet introduction, so the refrain would have more impact. The song pretty much alternates between the soft and loud sections, before exiting with a lengthy instrumental section of wordless 'aaah's' over Mellotron strings.

'E festa' ('Celebration') allows the band to rock out a bit – opening with swift piano arpeggios, followed by harmony guitar riffs, it turns into a glam rock stomp, with impressive fast guitar work from Mussida, a snakey Moog solo and a surprise piccolo lead break! Suddenly, everything slows down for a dreamy middle vocal section before taking off once again. Then it slows right down for a flute and guitar interlude before once again taking flight. Lyrically, it's all fairly simple, sparse stuff – 'it's a party, as always, it's the party. Whose is it?' Special mention must be made of Di Cioccio's frantic but beat-perfect drumming that drives the whole thing along. The band considered 'E Festa' to be the first rock tarantella – an Italian folk dance in a fast, upbeat tempo.

We then come to what PFM considered to be one of the most important tracks on the album. 'Dove...quando...' (Where or When?') follows the PFM template of a gentle opening based on finger-picked guitar with an almost mediaeval refrain and mournful lyrics, followed by a faster, piano-led instrumental in odd time signatures described as '15th-century jazz', as if Rick Wakeman had added a seventh track to his debut album *Six Wives of Henry VIII*, dedicated to the king's jester. Then there's a slow, majestic classical section, followed by what sounds like a variation on Dave Brubeck's 'Take 5' (although in 6/8, so Take 6), with flute improv on top.

It's a fascinating, unpredictable track that shows off many of the band's musical influences, marred only by the strange decision to split it in half and put the two parts on different sides of the album – play the CD or digital version and you hear it as it was intended to be heard.

The award-winning 'La carozza di Hans' comes next, PFM's first original song, composed by Di Cioccio as he drove from Turin to Milan with his sleeping friends in the car. Rushing home to his guitar, he completed it in just two hours and the band worked it up for the Viareggio Festival. Lyrically, it is intended to imply a man's travels through life – Hans is a merchant, his carriage (or coach) waiting to take him on his life's journey.

Opening with unaccompanied vocal, the track passes through several different sections: a Black Sabbath-like heavy rock riff matching the vocal melody; a pretty acoustic guitar-led tune in A minor that builds in instrumentation with flute and occasional percussion; a sparse, classical guitar interlude; and a fast strum in 6/8 with impressive classical guitar runs before violin takes over, with guitar and organ riffs underneath owing not a little to Jethro Tull, ending rather abruptly. It's an interesting track that displays all the band's skills and influences but is perhaps too disjointed to be anything other than a curiosity.

The album ends on the second track PFM really rate from this album, 'Grazie Davvero' (Thanks A Lot), which is notable for its wind orchestrations by Premoli. Indeed, at times the band sound like an orchestra, with punches of flute and brass and grand piano chords under strong ensemble vocals. There are the, by now, obligatory quieter sections but this is, in the main, a bold, triumphant number that ends the album on a high.

The band were delighted with the result, as were the record-buying public, who sent it to the top of the Italian charts for a week. Di Cioccio said on the band's website:

We recorded our first LP and we really liked it. We succeeded in finding our personal style and, even if our music sounded Italian, we felt we were ready to compete with the most famous international bands. We could find the right balance mixing synthesisers, electronic sounds, ancient mandolas and other unusual instrument sounds... And we created pure Italian progressive rock.

Despite the album's parochial success, PFM were, of course, still utterly unknown outside Italy except among a few of the prog-rock cognoscenti. After touring in theatres across the country, the band decided to rectify that situation by recording an album they hoped would give them the international breakthrough they craved. The result, *Per Un Amico* (For A Friend), is a more disciplined album, one that mixes their disparate influences with a bit more care and consideration. That's not to say it's dull and predictable – far from it. The Gentle Giant influence is still there in the sudden, mid-song changes in tempo and mood, but it all seems to hang together a little better rather than lurching from one genre to another.

Opening track 'Appena Un Po' ('Just a Little') shows what I mean – a dreamy, string-based introduction leads to solo classical guitar finger-picking, then turns into a Bach-like tune played on flute and harpsichord – think Jethro Tull's 'Bouree' from their 1969 LP, *Stand Up* – before jumping into a rocking instrumental section that could also have come from our friends in Tull. When the vocals come in, they are over acoustic guitar and flute, with subdued drumming and sparse bass, before Mellotron and guitar take us into swelling King Crimson 'Epitaph' territory.

But we're still only halfway through the song. There's a jig-like instrumental section reminiscent of something Mike Oldfield could have come up with on *Ommadawn* and a reprise of the gentle verses before stately Mellotron strings take us into a sudden musical breakdown to the end.

On paper, it sounds as if someone armed with a razor blade broke into the recording studio and sliced all the tapes up, leaving the band to try and splice it together as best they could. In reality, it all seems to hang together, creating an impressive, dramatic and unpredictable opening number.

Second track 'Generale!' ('General') ranks as one of the best prog instrumentals of the 1970s, an incredibly complex but thrilling composition that powers along almost non-stop – Di Cioccio sets things up with a jazzy drum intro in an impossible time signature before guitar and bass play a tricky riff under Keith Jarrett-like piano improvisations from Premoli. The track settles into a fairly straightforward rocker as Mussida improvises over the top on guitar, sounding remarkably like Steve Howe on 'The Gates of Delirium' (but two years earlier – I wonder if Howe ever heard this track?).

There's a sudden lurch into a piccolo marching tune and some swelling organ before we dive back into the tricky riff from earlier, fading out on the

71

Howe-like guitar sound. It's a track that has more packed into it than some bands manage in an entire album but, like 'Appena Un Po", still sounds cohesive right up to the very end.

The title track sticks to the PFM formula of gentle introductions, this time marrying flute and piano in a minor key until pulsating keyboard chords and slashing violin introduce the vocals. There's a lengthy instrumental section incorporating improvised violin over a piano, bass and drums backing that seems to go anywhere and everywhere at once, before fast major key strumming on guitar plays us out, repeating three chords under Moog synth lead before ending, rather bizarrely, with what sounds like a fanfare.

'Il Banchetto' ('The Feast') is a real treat, the closest PFM come to something you could actually sing along to (if you knew Italian, that is – the lyrics translate rather clumsily into 'Sir, Majesty, Everyone is here, reverent as usual. Sir, it's us: The Poet, The Murderer and His Holiness. All your faithful friends'). The verse melody is simple and effective, over alternating strummed chords in G major and D minor, but played up the neck of the guitar so they have a chiming sound to them.

Of course, this being PFM, the track eventually changes into something else, this time a lovely Moog solo in 6/8 over Genesis-like acoustic guitars. I love the way the bass bounces back and forth in this section, which builds in intensity and drama until... something completely different – it sounds to me like someone falling on the keys of a fairground pipe organ. Then there's a solo piano playing a kind of classical-jazz hybrid – I hate to keep making comparisons but think of a cross between Rick Wakeman in the middle of 'Heart of the Sunrise' and John Evan on Jethro Tull's 'By King Permission Of' from the *Living in the Past* compilation album. The song ends with a reprise of the catchy opening chords.

Finally, 'Geranio' ('Geranium') once again offers a gentle opening, this time of sombre piano chords and ghostly vocals, before we build up again into something more jazzy and exciting, almost 1960s in its simple, upbeat melody. That shifts suddenly into a dramatic, oom-pah-pah piano section, then a wash of pretty strings, then a bloody great gong before the return of the opening melody, this time played on pipe organ and acoustic guitar. It ends with a repeated three-note melody played on tubular bells!

I've tried my best to describe what I'm hearing, but, as someone once said (and nobody is sure who), writing about music is like dancing about architecture, particularly when the music is as playful and varied as this is. Once again, anyone thinking it sounds less of a feast, more like the contents of a restaurant's bins at the end of an evening, should think again – it really does work. This is partly due to the fact PFM were full of great musicians – Premoli's piano playing is astonishing, while Di Cioccio's drums hold everything together and the bass is locked in with them – and they come up with such great melodies, time and time again.

There's a reason why *Per Un Amico* has four and a half stars from Allmusic and frequently appears in the Top 20 of the greatest prog albums. Take a listen and you'll hear what I mean.

Strangely, the album did not do as well in the charts as its predecessor, but it would soon become known in a slightly different form in the important US and UK markets. Keith Emerson was given a tape of PFM's music and he attended a concert in Rome, immediately signing the band to ELP's newly-fledged record label, Manticore. PFM's first job was to create an English language version of *Per Un Amico*, which came out in 1973 as *Photos of Ghosts*. All the tracks were given new titles that didn't translate directly from the Italian, so 'Appena un po" became 'River of Life', 'Geranio' retitled as 'Promenade the Puzzle' and the original title track became the English album's title track, too.

Most of the songs were rerecorded with English vocals, although the instrumental 'Generale!' was left untouched, becoming instead 'Mr 9 Til 5', and 'Il Banchetto' was a remix. The album also contained 'E festa' from the debut album, which was retitled 'Celebration' and released as a single, and there was a newly-recorded instrumental called 'Old Rain'.

PFM are still performing and recording 52 years after they were formed, and are still regarded as Italy's finest progressive rock band and the first to achieve international success. Premiata, indeed!

Matching Mole – *Matching Mole*

Personnel
Bill MacCormick: bass guitar
Phil Miller: guitar
David Sinclair: piano, organ
Robert Wyatt: Mellotron, piano, drums, vocal
Recorded December 1971 to February 1972 at CBS Studios, London
Produced by Matching Mole
Recorded & engineered by Richard Dodd & Mike Fitzhenry
Label: CBS Records
Released date: 8 April
Chart places: did not chart
Tracks: 'O Caroline', 'Instant Pussy', 'Signed Curtain', 'Part of the Dance', 'Instant Kitten', 'Dedicated to Hugh, But You Weren't Listening', 'Beer as in Braindeer', 'Immediate Curtain'
All tracks written by Robert Wyatt except 'O Caroline' by Wyatt/Sinclair and 'Part of the Dance' by Miller.

The story so far...

Born in Bristol but living near Dover (and going to school in Canterbury), Wyatt was taught drums by visiting US jazzer George Neidorf. He became friends with Australian beatnik Daevid Allen, who lodged with his parents in 1961 and formed a trio with bass-playing friend Hugh Hopper. When Allen left, Wyatt and Hopper formed The Wilde Flowers with guitarist/vocalist Kevin Ayers, Richard Sinclair and Hugh's older brother Brian. Allen returned and the band split into two – half went on to form Caravan, while Wyatt, Allen, Ayers and keyboard-player, Mike Ratledge, formed The Soft Machine, named after the 1961 novel by William Burroughs. The Softs became, along with Pink Floyd, involved in the UK underground movement, playing at London clubs such as UFO. Their first single, 'Love Makes Sweet Music', was released and flopped in 1967. Allen left after being denied entry back into the UK following French appearances, leaving the band as a three-piece to record a debut album. Ayers left after a 1968 US tour supporting Jimi Hendrix, replaced by Hugh Hopper for a second album, imaginatively titled *Volume Two*. Their third album (called, wait for it, *Third*) added a horn section but showed a growing split between instrumental jazz and Wyatt's quirky songs. Wyatt recorded a solo album, *An End of an Ear*, before leaving Soft Machine following their all-instrumental album, *Fourth*.

The album

Robert Wyatt had hit rock bottom. Sacked by the band he loved, wracked with self-loathing, depressed by the state of his relationship and trying to drown his anxieties in bucketloads of booze, he finally attempted what he had been threatening to do for the last few weeks. In *Different Every Time: The Authorised Biography of Robert Wyatt*, by Marcus O'Dair, his then-partner Caroline Coon recalled: 'We'd gone back up to Hampstead from Ronnie Scott's and Rob was in a terrible state, having to be restrained. I think there was sick and blood – he might have cut his wrists. I stood back from the melee and this big black hole opened up before my eyes. It was really horrific'.

It was his lowest point in a life and career that has had more peaks and troughs than the rides at Alton Towers. It may have been even worse than that time a few years later when he fell out of a window and broke his back, putting him in a wheelchair for the rest of his life.

Wyatt was – and probably still is – a shy, deep, sensitive man suffering from a lack of self-worth, probably stemming from the fact that his father was a driven intellectual with degrees from both Oxford *and* Cambridge. The son definitely wasn't a chip off the old academic block, but he seemed to find himself, to discover his place in the world, in his music. As the drummer and one of the vocalists and composers in The Soft Machine, he embraced an avant-garde intellectualism that allowed him to pen songs that sounded more like conversations, performed with a plaintive, hesitant, vulnerable English accent. Steeped in jazz, world music and the more challenging 20th-century classical composers, his work was miles away from rock 'n' roll.

But he was also a powerful, inventive and restless drummer, prepared to perform with anyone who would have him, soaking up experiences and making connections that would serve him well later in his career. Open and impulsive, he wanted to be liked and took rejection deeply seriously. So when it all started to go wrong in Soft Machine, it sent Robert down into a black hole of booze and hopelessness.

You can hear the changes in the group through the first four albums. At first, they are a collective, working together, arranging each other's work, collaborating as equals. If anything, the defining sound of the first two Soft Machine albums is Wyatt's unique vocal phrasing. But by *Third*, Wyatt's contribution is limited to one side of a double album – and on 1971's *Fourth,* he was just the drummer, with no composing credit at all. Hopper and Ratledge rejected everything he offered, taking the group down an instrumental jazz-fusion path that had no place for a singing drummer.

And that hurt deeply. After all, he started it. He had brought them together – he'd got Hugh playing with Mike, and Elton Dean playing Mike's tunes. And now, they were trying to force him out of his own group. On one occasion, Wyatt burst into tears during a show in Amsterdam as his sense of alienation overwhelmed him. Then it all came to a head during a night of boozing at Ronnie Scott's jazz club in London. Hugh Hopper told *Mojo* magazine: '[Wyatt] said to someone, "I wish I could find another band". The rest of us leapt on it and said, "Right, go then"'. And that was that.

He tried to keep going, playing with Keith Jarrett's Centipede at the Royal Albert Hall, with the Berlin Jazz Festival, with Canadian pianist Paul Bley. But with a creative outlet denied to him and his personal relationships dissolving in a lake of booze, he climbed in a bath and slashed his wrists in a suicide attempt that put him in hospital. Perhaps only music could save him now.

Wyatt knew he had to put something together, something of his own that allowed him to do both songs and instrumentals, to sing and drum, and he needed people around him he knew and trusted and who would be in tune with his musical vision. So he reached out to David Sinclair, who was an old friend from The Wilde Flowers, had played keyboards on his solo album *The End of an Ear* and had recently left the other big Canterbury band, Caravan. Sinclair was hitch-hiking through Portugal until Wyatt sent him a telegram saying, 'Come back, your country needs you!'

When Sinclair returned to Blighty, Wyatt visited him at his home in Kent to listen to the keyboard player's latest compositions. One of them, a medium-paced ballad with a well-worn chord sequence used by hundreds of songs, usually G, D and E minor (although Sinclair's is in Db), particularly caught his ear and inspired him to write some touching, honest lyrics about his ex, Caroline Coon. 'If you call this sentimental crap, you'll make me mad', he sings. And, 'But you must admit we both thought we'd be man and wife' (although she denies ever giving him that impression!). Later, Wyatt claimed the song was about his break-up from his old band, and it's true that 'I love you still, Soft Machine' would scan but is not nearly as poetic.

Sinclair's involvement in Matching Mole was to be brief and, in hindsight, one suspects he did it more out of loyalty to Wyatt than to develop his own musical aspirations. After all, he had left Caravan because he wanted to pursue more song-based compositions (despite writing that band's side-long epic 'Nine Feet Underground' on 1971's *In the Land of Grey and Pink*). Yet here he was back in a group that wanted to create long-form improvised pieces.

For a guitarist, Wyatt turned to London-born Phil Miller, who was a member of Delivery along with brother Steve and drummer Pip Pyle. Wyatt probably met them while playing the London clubs and the various connections they all had meant they soon became part of the Canterbury scene. In fact, Steve Miller replaced Sinclair in Caravan when the latter left in 1971 and Wyatt introduced Pip Pyle to Daevid Allen, leading to a stint with Gong.

Miller had written tracks for Delivery and was an accomplished jazz-rock improviser, so he brought with him some compositions that ended up on the first Matching Mole album. He would later form Hatfield and the North and National Health, and his guitar playing would become as much a part of the Canterbury sound as the keyboards of Ratledge and Sinclair. Miller said a friend tipped him off that Wyatt was looking for a guitarist, so he got in touch and joined the rehearsals at the drummer's then-home in Notting Hill. Wyatt said he wanted Miller because he was 'the only guitarist who doesn't conceptually piss me off a bit. I agree with him about how to play guitar and I really don't with anyone else'.

Completing the quartet was Bill MacCormick, who had known Wyatt since about 1966 – both their mothers were teaching assistants at the same school. MacCormick had started off as a drummer but moved to the bass, forming Quiet Sun with future Roxy Music guitarist Phil Manzanera. That band had broken up around the same time that Wyatt was forced out of Soft Machine. In the liner notes for the 2012 reissue of the first Matching Mole album, MacCormick recalled:

I just got a call, as Robert tends to do in these circumstances, asking me to come around and do some playing to see what happens. We'd spend the entire time either talking about music or playing it, not to mention drinking copious cups of tea, as well as living on a diet of fried eggs on marmite and toast. That was Robert's favourite combination and we'd eat it for breakfast, lunch and dinner!

At that stage, no one was entirely sure what Wyatt's plan actually was, and likely or not, neither was he. At one stage, he was thinking of a solo album of love songs, which was why Sinclair's pretty tune appealed to him so much. But as the quartet ran through old Caravan numbers, Wyatt's Soft Machine epic, 'Moon in June', George Harrison's 'Beware of Darkness' and interesting musical ideas from Miller, things slowly began to come together. By October 1971, they had even settled on a name, a cheeky pun on the French translation of Soft Machine – machine molle, which became Matching Mole – and Wyatt even toyed with the idea of taking the gentle piss out of his former band's penchant for numbering its albums by suggesting his new group would release Soft Machine 1, Soft Machine 2 and so on.

Softs manager Sean Murphy got Matching Mole a record deal with CBS, who offered the band time in a studio off Oxford Street to record the debut album. It was not, said MacCormick, the most enjoyable of experiences. He explained:

The place was really run down. The tapes ran at variable speeds and it was cold. This was the time of the miners' strikes and there were power cuts on a regular basis. We were constantly being told we couldn't come in or we'd get there and the tape machine would be running slow or not even working. It was quite a pain.

Sinclair added in the Wyatt biography:

It was a very big studio and, as far as I remember, there was a little one-bar electric burner. One bar, about a foot long, of heat in the building. We were all huddled around that before doing takes, warming our hands, and then we'd rush off to our instruments and do the take. It was a little bit bizarre.

That's why there were actually three studios involved, the other two being Command in Piccadilly and Nova near Marble Arch. To add to his woes, someone stole MacCormick's treasured Fender Precision bass and he had to find a replacement at short notice. Thanks to all the obstacles placed in their path, Matching Mole didn't finish recording until March.

The result is an album that does precisely what Wyatt wanted it to do and was denied in Soft Machine. There are gentle songs that showcase his vulnerable vocals, and way-out improvised instrumentals that embark on a mysterious musical journey with no apparent destination. Opener 'O Caroline' lulls the listener into a false sense of predictable melodic security – it was that song Sinclair had written, with Wyatt's heartfelt lyrics about Caroline Coon. In fact, they are the only two musicians on the track – it was pretty much assembled in one night, with just Sinclair on keyboards and Wyatt on almost inaudible percussion. CBS chose it as a most unrepresentative single release, backed with another song that became track three on the album, the sparse and ironic 'Signed Curtain'.

Performed solely by Wyatt on hesitant but effective piano, it's another gentle ballad, even slower than 'O Caroline' but once again in the key of Db, with lyrics that appear to be an instruction manual on how to compose a song. 'This is the first verse', he sings in the first verse. Then, 'this is the chorus... or it might be a bridge... or just another part of the song that I'm singing'. After the second verse ('this is the second verse... might be the last verse'), Wyatt once again enters the chorus (or bridge) and then suggests it's 'just another key change' – immediately moving from a Gb major seventh chord to Eb. With that sense of hopelessness that seems to lurk in all his vocals, he resigns himself to finishing because 'it won't help me reach you'.

When I first heard the song, I thought he said 'retune', which seems to be a more apt ending when you attempt to play it and realise he *has* retuned, ending up in Gb minor, from which he could have easily gone back to Db. The melody was something Wyatt had hanging around since at least 1968 when he recorded a demo at the end of a Soft Machine tour with Jimi Hendrix under the title 'Chelsa' and with Daevid Allen sharing the credit. The new title was meant to emphasise that this was Wyatt's last pop song – the curtain was coming down and it was signed like an artist finishes a painting.

Two more tracks on the album showcase Wyatt's vocals, this time highlighting his ethereal, wordless scat singing. 'Instant Pussy' is a reworking of 'To Carla, Marsha and Caroline (For Making Life Beautifuller)' from his first solo album, *The End of an Ear* – the names refer to American jazz composer Carla Bley, novelist and singer Marsha Hunt, and Wyatt's long-suffering partner. On the original, Wyatt played piano and organ; on 'Instant Pussy', his repetitive four-note motif is replaced by MacCormick's bass, gentle jazz drumming, tasteful guitar and almost background keyboard contributions from Sinclair. It reaches a bit of crescendo before segueing seamlessly into 'Signed Curtain'. Oh, and it's in Db again. (Incidentally, the preponderance of flats on the album strongly suggests the recording was slowed down or sped up a semi-tone – why would you play half of side one in Db if you could have played it in C or D?).

'Instant Kitten', on side two, seems to take up where 'Pussy' left off, with more wordless scat over what sounds like organ chords recorded backwards before drums, bass and lead guitar come in for a more muscular, improved workout over a repetitive chord cycle of C minor, D major and F minor. There is a melody here that Sinclair keeps returning to on his Hammond organ and, in places, it sounds very much like his aforementioned 'Nine Feet Underground'. At about the four-minute mark, it appears to reach a natural end, except Wyatt continues for another minute or so, playing unaccompanied, discordant notes on his Mellotron.

The rest of the album consists of improvised band instrumentals, particularly the nine-minute side one closer, 'Part of the Dance', which was edited down from a 21-minute jam. Composed by Phil Miller, it is based on a staccato, tumbling eight-note motif and a loose chord sequence similar to 'Instant Kitten' but a semi-tone higher. Miller and Wyatt play with power and gusto, while Sinclair seems a little unsure of himself, offering sporadic stabs of Hammond organ.

Track two on side two, 'Dedicated to Hugh, But You Weren't Listening', is, it seems, a little dig at Hugh Hopper by Wyatt, perhaps about the fact that neither Hopper nor Ratledge were prepared to listen to anything Wyatt had composed in the dying days of his tenure with Soft Machine (there's a similar dig at Hopper in 'Memory Lain, Hugh' on Caravan's 1973 album, *For Girls Who Grow Plump in the Night*, supposedly alluding to a dispute over composing credits between Hopper and Pye Hastings). The title is almost identical to Hopper's composition on Soft Machine's *Volume Two*, a quirky song sung by Wyatt with mostly solo acoustic guitar finger-picked backing. Wyatt's composition is a disturbing minor key improv based mainly on two alternating chords that segues into 'Beer as in Braindeer', which is four minutes of everyone pretty much playing whatever they want in whatever key they fancy. It is a testing piece of music, to say the least!

That, in turn, merges into 'Immediate Curtain', a sound collage with even fewer tunes in it but with Mellotron backing that sounds like King Crimson doing Holst's Mars, the Bringer of War. Eventually, the Mellotron is on its own, ending with a long, drawn-out, doom-laden chord – C minor with an added ninth, I think, but don't quote me on that.

Matching Mole's challenging, uncommercial debut was released in April 1972 with an amusing and eye-catching cover showing two identical, bespectacled moles facing each other. It received rave reviews from *Melody Maker* ('they cut to ribbons almost any band you could think of') and the *New Musical Express* ('devastates anything by the corporate cool smoothie the Soft Machine'), although some reviewers criticised the schizophrenic nature of the album in its mixture of gentle ballads and way-out improv.

Hindsight places it among the pantheon of great Canterbury releases, not least because it has the eclectic feel of a Robert Wyatt solo album, and he is now quite rightly revered by Canterbury music fans. Matching Mole's second album was more of a group affair, although the line-up went through one important change with the departure of Sinclair, who really, really didn't want to do this jazz stuff any more. He was replaced by Dave MacRea, who had actually helped out on the first album but to what extent is known only by the musicians. He made his debut only days after the album was released, appearing on a BBC Radio One John Peel session on 17 April.

Sadly, Matching Mole proved to be a short-lived chapter in Wyatt's story. A third album was in the offing until he plunged from a fourth-floor window during a birthday party for Daevid Allen's wife, Gilli Smyth, and was left a paraplegic for the rest of his life. But, thankfully, Wyatt reached *Rock Bottom* – the title of his second solo album in 1974 that set him on the path to becoming one of Britain's most-loved musical eccentrics.

Frank Zappa and the Mothers – *The Grand Wazoo*

Personnel
Frank Zappa: vocals, guitar
...and a load of other people. I mean, loads of them
Recorded April to May 1972 at Paramount Studios, Hollywood
Produced by Frank Zappa
Engineered by Kerry McNabb
Burritos by Ernie's Taco House
Label: Bizarre/Reprise
Released 27 November 1972
Chart places: US: did not chart, UK: did not chart
Tracks: 'For Calvin (And His Next Two Hitch-Hikers)', 'The Grand Wazoo', 'Cletus
Awreetus-Awrightus', 'Eat That Question', 'Blessed Relief'
All tracks written by Frank Zappa (the first two tracks are switched around for
later Ryko CD release)

The story so far...

Born in Baltimore, Maryland, in 1940, Frank Zappa was a precociously
intelligent young man who was inspired by RnB and doo-wop, the modernist
classical music of Igor Stravinsky and the sound experiments of Edgard Varese.
Beginning his musical career as a drummer, he switched to guitar, moved
to Los Angeles and tried to make a living as a composer and producer. He
was briefly imprisoned after recording a fake erotic audio tape with a female
friend. In 1965, he took control of local band The Soul Giants, calling them
The Mothers. They were spotted by record producer Tom Wilson, who signed
them to Verve/MGM Records, renaming them The Mothers of Invention. Their
debut, *Freak Out!*, was only the second rock double album. Between 1966 and
1971, Zappa released no fewer than twelve albums, including *We're Only in it
For the Money*, with its *Sgt Pepper*-pastiche cover; the UK hit, *Hot Rats*; and the
film and accompanying soundtrack album, *200 Motels*.

The album

The show had been going so well. The band – an incarnation of The Mothers
formed back in June 1970 with Howard Kaylan and Mark Volman, otherwise
known as The Turtles – had just finished the first encore, a cover of The
Beatles' hit 'I Want to Hold Your Hand'. Just six days earlier, in Montreux,
Switzerland, the encore had been interrupted by cries of 'Fire!' as the theatre
began to burn down, an event immortalised in the Deep Purple song 'Smoke
on the Water', beloved of amateur guitarists everywhere (duh, duh, duh... duh,
duh, du-duh).

But at London's Rainbow Theatre on 10 December 1971, there seemed
no reason why the band shouldn't finish the show unscathed and continue
its European tour. After 'I Want to Hold Your Hand', everyone left the stage

again and then Zappa came out to announce the next encore. Long-time fan Howard Thompson, quoted in Neil Slaven's Zappa biography *Electric Don Quixote*, recalled:

> Suddenly out of the corner of my eye, I saw this guy run down to the orchestra pit, leap over it onto stage right, run across about five feet to where Zappa was standing and just shove him. And Zappa tumbled into the orchestra pit, right in front of me. I leaned over the barrier and looked down into the pit, which was about fifteen feet below the stage. Zappa was just lying there prone.

In the same book, Mark Volman said:

> I remember looking down at him from the top of the pit and his leg was bent underneath him like a Barbie doll; his eyes were open, but there was no life in them. Two or three of us were cradling him in the pit and the blood was running from his head to his knees. We weren't sure if he would live through the night.

His attacker, 24-year-old Trevor Charles Howell of Walthamstow, London, later claimed in court that he had assaulted Zappa because he wasn't giving 'value for money', although the real reason was probably because his then-girlfriend had a crush on the musician. Whatever the motivation for his unprovoked assault, Zappa was left with a broken ankle, a broken rib, a crushed larynx and a paralysed arm. It looked like the show was over for the foreseeable future.

A lesser man than Zappa may have seen this as a sign to slow down. After all, in less than six years, he had released twelve albums (thirteen if you include *King Kong: Jean-Luc Ponty Plays the Music of Frank Zappa*), made a movie and toured almost non-stop, only taking breaks to write and record. No one would have blamed him for metaphorically and literally putting his feet up in his wheelchair and living off his royalties for a while.

But relaxing his restless musical mind was easier said than done, and by February, he was already planning new projects. It seemed clear the attack heralded the end of the last Mothers line-up – they couldn't afford to sit around waiting for Zappa to heal, so they drifted off into other bands or, in the case of Kaylan and Volman, signed record deal as a duo, Flo & Eddie. (Mildly interesting sidenote: The names came from their onstage characters in The Mothers' show – Volman was Flo and Kaylan was Eddie. But the cover of their first album printed the wrong names under their pictures! So they just swapped identities ...).

As a swansong, Zappa took some live recordings (he recorded *everything*, including his bandmates saying, 'I bet he's recording us right now') and released *Just Another Band From LA* in May 1972, documenting part of the

1971 tour that included sharing the stage at New York's Fillmore East with John Lennon and Yoko Ono (later released on the couple's album *Some Time in New York City*). It included the 24-minute epic 'Billy the Mountain', about a peak that finally receives its royalties for all the picture postcards and decides to go on vacation with wife Ethel, a tree growing out of its shoulder, crushing many towns and cities along the way.

By the time he was able to play guitar again, Zappa was back in the studio to record a follow-up to his critically acclaimed 1969 album *Hot Rats*. With no fewer than fifteen musicians, including trumpets, trombones, tenor saxes, pedal steel guitar and 'electric bed springs' (played by Zappa), the result was an eclectic mixture of big band jazz over Miles Davis-style rock backing. *Hot Rats 2: Waka/Jawaka*, released in July 1972, was not as well received as its predecessor and is a minor entry in his canon.

Undeterred, Zappa took some other tracks recorded during those sessions to fashion the album that I have chosen as his best of 1972 and one that is an essential part of every music lover's collection. *The Grand Wazoo* was a title Zappa had hanging around from 1969 – it was a reference to the Grand Masters in freemasonry, and the fact they are usually just jumped-up shop owners with silly hats and meaningless scrolls.

For the album of that name, Zappa created a bizarre story about an alternate universe based on Ancient Rome, ruled over by the Funky Emperor, Cletus Awreetus-Awrightus, who has an army of unemployed musicians that fights weekly battles with the Mediocrates of Pedestrium. Cletus also has to deal with a new cult of music-hating fanatics known as Questions – using a megaphone called The Grand Wazoo, he questions the Questions, and anyone who can play an instrument is allowed to join his army. The rest are consumed in a tank of Undifferentiated Tissue, whatever that is...

Like many of Zappa's creations, particularly the non-musical ones, it was a combination of pointed political comment, sideswipes at the music industry and extreme silliness. The Questions were originally Christians, showing Zappa's disdain for the emerging religious fanaticism of the American right wing that has now led to a complete evangelist takeover of the Republican Party. Artist Cal Schenkel, who had started working with Zappa in 1967 and was adept at converting his crazy ideas into deeply intricate and visually exciting artwork, fashioned a cover that showed a battle in the middle of ancient Rome but with all the 'soldiers' wielding instruments instead of weapons. There is no attempt here to be historically accurate – some of the army wear Norman helmets, while Zappa is portrayed as a Pharoah playing electric guitar. The back cover shows an elderly 'Uncle Meat' (a reference to an earlier Zappa album) conjuring up the alternate universe in his secret laboratory.

Being mostly instrumentals, the tracks on *The Grand Wazoo* could have been called anything and appear to have received their names largely thanks to the story in the record sleeve. For example, 'The Grand Wazoo' itself was originally called 'Think it Over' and started life as an aria in a science fiction musical called Hunchentoot Zappa had written while convalescing – he had the book, the lyrics and even designed the costumes but it was never staged. In the aria, a 'religious fanatic conman of the future' tells his followers how to overcome any obstacle, singing: 'If something gets in your way, think it over, and it will fall down'.

Initial rehearsals for *Waka/Jawaka* and *The Grand Wazoo* albums show that Zappa intended at first to keep the lyrics but eventually ditched them to create what he called 'just a shuffle' – albeit one that lasts nearly fourteen minutes. He is being a bit self-deprecating here – recorded with no fewer than nineteen musicians, it does indeed start as a mean, bouncy shuffle in D minor with Zappa's lead guitar over the top. But after about one and a half minutes, we hear the 'Think it Over' melody played by the brass before a triumphant fanfare-like blast leads back into the D minor shuffle. As always with Zappa, there's much more going on here with the brass section, his own superb, biting guitar-playing, a sleazy trombone solo by Billy Byers, Don Preston from the original Mothers on Minimoog and bottleneck slide guitar by Tony Duran. Sal Marquez also plays wah-wah trumpet that sounds like a little voice nagging at you, while Mothers' drummer Aynsley Dunbar thrashes the hell out of his kit.

Even though most of the track is on the one chord, Zappa keeps interest and excitement going throughout with blasts of magnificent melody and changes in tempo. Those who compare *The Grand Wazoo* and its predecessor to the 1970s work of Miles Davis need to know there is more going on in fourteen minutes of Zappa music than in all of Davis's 'cop show funk' period.

The title track was originally the second on the album – the opener was 'For Calvin (and His Next Two Hitch-Hikers)', but they were swapped on Zappa's instructions for the CD release and have remained that way ever since. Right decision because the latter tune is more introspective and lacks 'The Grand Wazoo"s impressive punch. 'For Calvin...' has vocals that reference a real-life event in the life of illustrator Schenkel. In a 1995 interview quoted on the *killuglyradio.com* website, he recalled:

My 39 Pontiac was in the shop, so I had borrowed a car from Frank. It was this 1959 white Mark VIIII Jaguar that used to belong to Captain Beefheart... I just left Frank's house and I'm stopped at the corner of Mulholland and Laurel Canyon Blvd, waiting for a red light to change, when I notice these two hitchhikers: a hippie couple standing there waiting for a ride. The next thing I know, they are getting in the back of the car. I guess they must have thought I offered them a ride (I didn't tell them to come into my car or motion them or anything – I wasn't even thinking of it), so I ask them where they are going and they didn't say ANYTHING! I drive down Laurel Canyon Blvd past the Log Cabin, past Harry Houdini's, past the country store and into Hollywood. I get to the bottom of the hill, I was going to turn right. I

kind of asked them 'look I'm turning right, do you want to get out here?'
They didn't say anything. They were just blank. I figured they were on acid
or something. I just couldn't communicate with them. I wasn't sure what to
do, so I just continued on to my destination. When I get there I said, 'OK,
this is where I'm going. Goodbye!' They just stayed in the car and didn't get
out. So I parked the car, got out and went up to my studio ... Every once in
a while, I'd look out of the window to see if they were gone, but they were
still sitting in the back seat of the car. An hour or two later, I looked out
the window and I noticed they were gone. I thought, 'finally!' Then shortly
afterwards, I saw that they were back! They went to the supermarket for a
loaf of bread and lunchmeat and started making sandwiches in the back of
the car. They were eating their lunch! Then they left.

There are about eleven lines of lyrics that reference the episode, asking,
'Where did they go? Where did they come from?', sung by Sal Marquez and
Janet Neville-Ferguson over a moody, waltz-time backing before the tune
seems to slowly disintegrate into mysterious random brass and percussion
noises that perhaps depict the two stoned hippies munching their sandwiches
in the car. There's a brief and totally out-of-place reference to a tune called
'New Brown Clouds', a sort of parping marching tune on trombone, that
would later form part of a longer work called 'The Adventures of Greggery
Peccary'. At about the four-minute mark, there is a flurry of improvised
instrumentation before plunging into an atonal piece of avant-garde jazz (as
in, I avant-garde a clue what's going on), once again led mostly by trombone.
The final few minutes of brass and woodwind interplay are some of the most
'out there' jazz Zappa has written, but it all holds together beautifully until
the end.

The title of 'Cletus Awreetus-Awrightus' was inspired by 1950s blues shouter
Big Joe Turner's catchphrase 'All right then! All reet then!' As we know,
Cletus is the funky ruler of the imaginary Ancient Roman land of Zappa's
imagination, and the music is suitably funky too, opening with a triumphant
fanfare blast of brass, swooping percussion and George Duke playing fierce
and furious arpeggios. There are tunes galore here as they tumble over
each other in quick succession. It settles down into a pumping rhythm with
Duke playing what sounds like saloon-bar piano, followed by Ken Shroyer's
'multiple trombones' jumping about as if they are on fire.

Then we get a restatement of the fanfare but with vocals – not lyrics as
such, but playful la-las and rum-pum-poms from Zappa, backed up in a
higher register by Duke and singer Lauren Wood (aka Chunky), before a big
finish from the whole band. It is one of the finest three minutes ever recorded
and the standout track from the album.

'Eat That Question' – originally, of course, 'Eat That Christian' – opens with
George Duke on keyboards. Duke, now sadly gone, was a phenomenal
musician whose recording career started in 1966 and came to Zappa's attention

during a gig as part of violinist Jean-Luc Ponty's band. In an interview with John Kirby, published posthumously online in 2020, he explained:

> I found out that Quincy Jones was in the audience, Frank Zappa, and all these people; there were a lot of musicians in the area who wanted to see this electric violinist, not me. So I said, 'Something tells me this is a shot for me'. I decided that I was going to become very extroverted and play. It was almost like a basketball player saying to himself, 'Okay, this is my time to step up'. I started playing with my feet, I started playing with my elbows – I practically stood on that keyboard. I didn't know much about the electric piano, but I turned a few knobs and found out that you could get a vibrato. And Frank liked it. Frank said, 'Oh, well, this guy is nuts!' So he hired me.

Duke joined Zappa for eleven albums between 1970 and 1979, returning for *Them or Us* in 1984, and praised him for up-ending his serious approach to music. On 'Eat That Question', he opens with a flurry of electric piano notes, starting low before building up until he introduces the bluesy refrain that provides the backbone of the tune. He improvises practically all the way through, sometimes as little more than a trio with Dunbar on drums and Erroneous, aka Alex Dmochowsk, on drums. Zappa is playing guitar and percussion on this, while Marquez adds 'multiple toots' on brass. It's a frantic, spirited performance by the smallest ensemble on the album and reflects, perhaps, the part of the story when the music-hating Questions are being thrown into the tank of Undifferentiated Tissue (a concept borrowed – or Burroughed – from William Burroughs' book, *Naked Lunch*).

About a minute from the end, the entire band crashes into the bluesy refrain that Duke introduced, with Dunbar playing a marching beat underneath, making it all sound rather militaristic. It is one of only two tracks on the album that fade out.

This is the second, a serene jazz waltz that may come as a 'Blessed Relief' to anyone who found the preceding four tracks a little challenging – indeed, that may be why Zappa gave it that title. Opening with a gentle keyboard and bass vamp in Bbmaj7, it moves into F for a gentle melody that could almost be Burt Bacharach, led by Marquez playing a beautiful, soulful solo on trumpet. Duke takes a solo on electric piano before Zappa finishes up with some very tasteful jazz guitar, showing once again what a master he is of his instrument.

The Grand Wazoo was virtually ignored on release (except by Zappa fanatics, of course) but has been belatedly reassessed as one of the highpoints of his catalogue, a memorable and melodic album that is almost – but not quite – as good as *Hot Rats*. Not only that, it helped get him back on stage after the attack at the end of 1971 – he put together a 20-piece orchestra to play pieces from his three jazz-rock albums, along with the newly-composed 'The Adventures of Greggery Peccary'.

It was the start of a new phase in Zappa's career that was to last another 20 years, virtually right up to his death in 1994. During that time, he released another 46 albums, with countless others appearing posthumously, reviving The Mothers of Invention for one last hurrah in 1973.

The attack by Trevor Howell could have ended his career. Instead, it inspired him to even greater heights. So, in a way, we should be thankful to the jealous young man who knocked Zappa off the stage all those years ago. On second thoughts – let's not.

Neu! – *Neu!*

Personnel:
Michael Rother: guitar, bass guitar, bowed bass
Klaus Dinger: drums, guitar, Japan banjo, vocals
Recorded December 1972 at Star Studios, Hamburg
Produced and engineered by Konrad 'Conny' Plank and Neu!
Label: Brain Records
Release date: March 1972
Chart places: UK: did not chart, US: did not chart
Tracks: 'Hallogallo', 'Sonderangebot', 'Weissensee', 'Im Gluck', 'Negativland',
'Lieber Honig' All tracks by Dinger and Rother

The story so far...

Dinger, the son of a carpenter from Westphalia, Germany, practised hitting
bits of wood before he could afford a drum kit. Forming and joining various
groups during the 1960s, he was invited to join the newly-created Kraftwerk
and played on side two of the band's 1970 debut album. Needing a guitarist,
Kraftwerk enlisted Rother, from Hamburg, who had also been educated in
England and Pakistan and was then a member of Spirits of Sound. Both left
Kraftwerk in 1971 to form their own band, Neu!

The album

According to Brian Eno, there were three great beats in the 1970s: Fela Kuti's
Afrobeat, James Brown's funk and Klaus Dinger's NEU-beat. Of these, Eno
said the latter – translated as 'New' but pronounced 'Noy' – were the world's
most important rock group.

Be that as it may, it is certainly true the band had an influence that far
outweighed its commercial success, and drummer Dinger is credited with
pioneering a minimalist four-to-the-bar rhythm with an almost mechanical
precision and simplicity. He wasn't a great drummer – in fact, he was quite
primitive in a natural, untaught way. Jazzy percussion in tricky-dicky time
signatures was beyond him – he was a no-nonsense, head-down, powerful
4/4 rhythm maker. In other words, Dinger was the first human drum machine.

It was not always so. Rother remembers during one Kraftwerk concert
that Dinger was such a manic drummer that he had cut himself on a broken
cymbal and blood was squirting everywhere. But a failed relationship with a
Swedish girl in 1971 led Dinger to attempt to seek solace in the drums, and
in particular, to play as if he was creating an unstoppable heartbeat, repetitive
and monotonous, pining for his lost love. Dinger called it 'Apache beat' as if
he was channelling the spirit of Native American percussion, but in Germany,
they coined a more industrial name for it: Motorik.

Dinger and Rother met when they were both asked to join an early
incarnation of Kraftwerk. Rother's first loves were the Sixties bands from

the UK – The Beatles, The Kinks, The Who and Cream – but, like a lot of rebellious German youth, he wanted to create something new, a Central European music that was free of the blues.

Kraftwerk – formed in Dusseldorf in 1970 by Ralf Hutter and Florain Schneider – were part of the German experimental music scene that *Melody Maker* mischievously dubbed 'krautrock'. None of the krautrockers liked the name, but it stuck. We now know the band for its minimalist, pulsating, industrial electronic music, particularly on commercially successful albums such as 1975's *Autobahn*. But in those early days, the band used more traditional rock instruments, including real drummers, and created looser jams that owed more to Can. The band were three-quarters through their debut album when their drummer quit and Dinger was approached by Hutter to fill the gap, playing on the fourth track, 'Von Himmel Hoch (From Heaven Above)'.

After extensive touring, Hutter suddenly quit Kraftwerk, leaving the band without a guitarist, so they poached Rother from Spirits of Sound (a band that would supply other Kraftwerk members) and they settled down as a fairly stable trio, occasionally pulling in Schneider's former bandmate, Eberhard Kranemann, on bass. The music they created on stage is seen as the prototype for what would become Neu! – there is footage on YouTube of Kraftwerk on German TV show, *Beat Club*, performing what became known as 'Truckstop Gondolier', eleven long minutes of improvised noise and random percussion that eventually settles into a driving rock beat in the same chord throughout before degenerating back into random weirdness. It was unlike anything Kraftwerk would later create.

Rother remembers exciting, explosive concerts with Kraftwerk, including the one in which the manic Dinger had cut himself on broken cymbals and was spraying blood all over the place. But it all went horribly wrong when the band went into the studio to record a follow-up. Somehow, the trio couldn't transfer the live chemistry into the sterile atmosphere of the recording studio, and it was clear they couldn't continue to work together. Dinger and Schneider were both spiky individuals who frequently clashed in the studio and, occasionally, their arguments could get quite nasty. It was clear a split was on the cards. In a 2022 interview for *The Life of the Record* podcast, Rother said:

It was easier for me to imagine working with Klaus [Dinger], although he was quite a different personality, to be honest. He had traits that made it impossible for me to consider him a friend. But as an artistic collaborator, he was just incredible, so we thought we should give it a try and work as a duo. We booked a studio with Conny Plank and we tried to record what we could deliver, and so that's what we did. Conny was immediately enthusiastic.

Konrad 'Conny' Plank was a German record producer who had hand-built his own 56-channel mixing desk at a time when few studios had graduated beyond sixteen. He produced the first Kraftwerk album and immediately saw the possibilities of putting Dinger and Rather together in a studio and seeing what happened. Without Conny, Dinger admits, Neu! may not have happened as the musicians had limited knowledge of how to record and produce an album.

The duo wanted to avoid any outside influence from a record company, so they put up the money themselves for the recording costs (Plank also put in a share) and gave away their publishing rights. They could only afford four sessions, and they worked at night because it was cheaper. According to Rother, none of the music they had tried out with Kraftwerk ended up being used for Neu! – in fact, the musicians didn't even rehearse. Rother had one or two melodies like 'Weissensee' and 'Im Glück' and the idea of one track that 'goes to the horizon', like 'Hallogallo'.

According to Dinger, the first few nights were a washout – things didn't start to gel until he brought in his Japanese banjo, also known as a taishogoto, which was used on the first track to be recorded, 'Negativland' (Rother says maybe he was right, or maybe the truth was slightly different!). But most of the basic tracks were laid down by Klaus on drums and Rother on guitar, and they had no real plan for what overdubs should be done.

Rother tried to create what he called 'clouds' – melodies that ebbed and flowed on top as the 'vehicle' surged along on its Motorik rails. With no real plan, the duo were blessed with lucky accidents, such as perfectly-pitched feedback and unintended guitar effects. Then Conny turned the tape around and recorded things backwards, just to see what it sounded like. Rother said in the podcast:

We somehow managed to get music on tape. We could have easily failed; it was a matter of luck, with enough music on the tape to release as the first Neu! album. These days, if I listen to a track like 'Hallogallo', which still has, for me, so much mystery, it's like a cat – I look at it and I think, yeah, it's really good. The things Conny put together, the remixed guitars, the backwards, forwards guitars, that was a great job and so impressive because I couldn't imagine myself being able to memorise all those parts.

The first appearance of Dinger's Motorik or Apache beat appears the instant you place the needle on side one of the album – along with Rother's guitar notes, it comes surging out of the speakers like a runaway steam train. But it's more organic – or organik – than you might think. There's a warmth to the drumming, with few hard edges, and even a hint of the Bo Diddley shuffle. There's an additional percussion sound, perhaps Rother hitting the muted strings of his guitar as well as providing sparse, rhythmic notes and long, languid, spacey solos over the top.

This is 'Hallogallo (Wild Partying)', one of the songs that 'goes to the horizon'. What Rother is saying is that it appears to have no musical destination – there are no lyrics, no verses, no chorus, just an endless stream of rhythm and notes in the single chord of E major, stretching endlessly on. Boring? Well, possibly. But here's the thing – it starts interesting, becomes boring, then becomes interesting again, purely through its sheer hypnotic relentlessness. It does sound as if it's going to the horizon – and on a spherical planet, the horizon is never reached.

Of course, it has to end at some point, and the band decided nine minutes and 47 seconds was enough, fading it out on Rother's slashing chords. It's followed by a more ambient piece, 'Sonderangebot (Special Offer)', in which electronically-treated cymbals, played by Dinger using a bow, whoosh in and out and droning sounds ebb to and fro as Rother plays atonal, Fripp-ish guitar lines over the top – he used a bottle of guitar cleaning fluid to create a slide effect. The whole thing is drenched in phasing, making it all float around like a cloud of music.

'Weisensee (White Lake)' also opens with a slow crash of cymbals and a drone, but Dinger is playing a steady, laid-back drum beat while Rother's guitar alternates between the chords of D and C (mostly). It builds up a bit before crashing into G major and back into D, with some tasty fuzz guitar over the top. The drone was created by Rother tuning all the strings of his guitar to D and then once again utilising his bottle, along with bowed bass guitar. The simple, almost innocent melody was something Rother had had in his head for a while – the softly-stroked chords are, according to Rother, like breathing in and out, or like a confusing waterfall.

Side two opens with some sound effects – there are oars in the water and a woman and a man in muted discussion. These were recorded by Dinger while visiting his girlfriend Anita in Norway (her father had moved the family there to get her away from the drummer) and they are clearly messing about in a rowing boat. The recordings would surface on several later songs, too, as their on-off relationship continued through the next few years.

On the track 'Im Gluck (Lucky)', the sound effects merge almost imperceptibly into a buzzy drone that goes on for about six minutes before the sound effects return. And, er, that's it, apart from a pretty seven-note guitar phrase that sounds like a distant seagull. There's a certain menace about the track, inspired perhaps by Dinger's frustration at being separated from the woman he loved by her parents.

That frustration is more violently expressed in 'Negativland (Negative Land)', the first track to be recorded, which opens rather starkly with the sound of a jackhammer used in road construction, hammering away with the addition of echoed voices and audience applause. This turns into what sounds like a jet engine before Dinger sets up a steady rock beat to Rother's equally steady bass. Rother said:

It also happened to me that the parents of my girlfriend were not happy about me, but in the case of Klaus Dinger, he had this anger that, in his case, led to amazing creativity... The jackhammer was just some sound source we found in the studio. I think it was included to disrupt the harmony of 'Im Gluck', the joyful boat ride Klaus shared with his girlfriend, and suddenly the disruption of this joy.

Once again, Plank adds phasing to the sounds, standing between two tape machines in the studio and slowing down one of them simply by putting his hand on the reel and letting go at the right moment. Now, there's supposed to be an electronically-treated Japanese banjo on here but, once again, the manual phasing changes it into an angry wall of sound that drifts across Dinger's drums and Rother's bass. This is the most 'industrial' track on the album – harsh, mechanical, intense and almost overwhelming. At times, the drumming stops and then restarts, faster than before, then reverts back to its original tempo.

Finally, 'Lieber Honig (Dear Honey)' ends the album with an actual song. Over sparse notes that sound more like a Japanese banjo than anything on 'Negativland', Dinger sings a rather dreary, almost strangled, vocal, presumably dedicated to Anita because the rowing boat sound effects make a return, mixed into a mournful drone. The guitar here is a twelve-string (with one missing) played by Dinger, and his vocal, performed at the same time, sounds as if he's in pain – it breaks and cracks with emotion. It is a difficult listen, not least because Dinger simply cannot sing, but is an open and honest recording that puts humanity into the album.

With 44 minutes of music on tape, Dinger and Rother were ready to release an LP. But what to call the band? It was Dinger who came up with the name Neu! – Rother didn't like it; he wanted something a bit more organic. Quoted on the band's Wikipedia entry, Dinger explained:

It was a protest against the consumer society but also against our 'colleagues' on the Krautrock scene who had totally different taste/styling, if any. I was very well informed about Warhol, pop art, contemporary art. I had always been very visual in my thinking. Also, during that time, I lived in a commune and in order to get the space that we lived in, I set up an advertising agency which existed mainly on paper. Most of the people that I lived with were trying to break into advertising so I was somehow surrounded by this Neu! all the time.

The band's Warholian logo – a big, bold word in red, complete with an exclamation mark – reflected this thinking, and certainly stood out on the record racks when it was released in Germany on Brain Records, helping Neu!'s debut to sell 35,000 copies – not bad for an underground album. Sadly, it was virtually ignored for the next 30 years until it was re-issued by a label founded by German singer Herbert Gronemeyer. Since then, it has been re-evaluated as 'krautrock's defining relentless rhythm' (*Q magazine*) and 'a landmark of German experimental rock' (*The New York Times*), as well as being cited as major influences by such rock luminaries as Brian Eno and David Bowie.

Dinger and Rother had a difficult relationship that lasted just two more albums and a brief reformation in the 1980s – perhaps Dinger's claim that he had experienced '1,000 LSD trips' had something to do with the fact that he seemed to alienate a lot of people he worked with. But even now, Rother cherishes the time they played together, and particularly the combination of luck and inspiration that created one of 1972's most original and influential progressive rock albums.

The Strawbs – *Grave New World*

Personnel
David Cousins: vocals, guitars, electric-acoustic dulcimer, recorders
John Ford: bass, vocals, acoustic guitar
Tony Hooper: vocals, acoustic guitar, autoharp
Richard Hudson: drums, vocals
Blue Weaver: organ, piano, Mellotron, harmonium, clavioline
Recorded November 1971 mainly at Morgan Studios but also at Island Studios
and Landsdowne Studios, all in London
Produced by The Strawbs
Engineered by Tom Allom (Morgan), Frank Owen (Island) and John Macksmith
(Landsdowne)
Label: A&M
Release date: February 1972
Chart places: UK: 11
Tracks: 'Benedictus', 'Hey, Little Man...Thursday's Child', 'Queen of Dreams',
'Heavy Disguise', 'New World', 'Hey Little Man...Wednesday's Child', 'The Flower
and the Young Man', 'Tomorrow', 'On Growing Older', 'Ah Me, Ah My', 'Is it
Today, Lord?', 'The Journey's End'
All tracks by Cousins except 'Heavy Disguise' by Ford, 'Tomorrow' by Cousins,
Hooper, Ford, Weaver, Hudson, 'Ah Me, Ah My' by Hooper, 'Is it Today, Lord?' by
Hudson and 'The Journey's End' by Cousins, Weaver.

The story so far...

The band was formed in 1964 by Cousins, Hooper and mandolin player
Arthur Phillips as The Strawberry Hill Boys, named after the area of
Twickenham, London, where they rehearsed, playing folk and bluegrass.
Cousins and Hooper opened their own folk club, The White Bear, at
Hounslow, London, where they began incorporating self-penned material
into their act. Having lost Phillips, they recruited double bass player Ron
Chesterman and were persuaded to shorten their name to The Strawbs
because it fit better on posters. They hooked up with young female folk
singer Sandy Denny, recording the first version of folk-rock classic 'Who
Knows Where the Time Goes' in Cousins' front room. Demo tapes clinched
them a deal with Denmark's Sonet Records and they recorded an album
on a cinema stage in Copenhagen during the day while playing locally at
night. But Denny left, so the album remained in the vaults for five years
before being released as *All Our Own Work*. Meanwhile, the Copenhagen
tapes persuaded A&M to offer a new contract and the band released first
single 'Oh How She Changed' in 1968 (originally recorded when Polydor
expressed an interest). For the debut album, The Strawbs recorded with Elton
John producer Gus Dudgeon (who was then Hooper's flatmate). Both the
single and album failed to chart. Second album *Dragonfly*, released in 1970,
featured short-lived new member, cellist Clare Deniz, and session musician

Rick 'One-Take' Wakeman on one track, 'Vision of the Lady of the Lake'. Wakeman joined, Chesterman left, cellist/bassist Lindsay Cooper came and went, bass player Ford and drummer Hudson were recruited. A concert at Queen Elizabeth Hall in London gave the band their first charting album in 1970, *Just A Collection Of Antiques And Curios*, thanks to the performance of pianist Wakeman, dubbed 'Tomorrow's Superstar'. Their follow-up, *From the Witchwood*, was recorded in early 1971, but issues arose with Wakeman, who was in a dire financial situation and needed to do session work to make ends meet. He may – or may not – have started working with Yes. Wakeman's predicted departure occurred just a few months later.

The album

Dave Cousins thought it was all over when Rick Wakeman left. He didn't do it face-to-face or with an apologetic phone call. It was a message sent through the band's manager: I'm off to join Yes, see you around the clubs. Or words to that effect. He later told *Jazz Weekly*:

> What happened was that we did a show in the North of England in Hull City Hall, sharing the bill with Yes. While we were playing, they were standing on the side watching Rick, and they decided they wanted Rick in the band. While we were making the *Witchwood* album, Rick was rehearsing with Yes at the same time. He didn't turn up in the studio all of the time; he kept disappearing until it leaked out what he was doing. Before the album came out, Rick had already left the band. He joined Yes, and six weeks later, our album came out. They were making *Fragile* at that time. They claim they made the album in those six weeks, but if you look at the timelines at the back of the albums, you can work it out. It's impossible for them to have recorded it after our album came out. It's very interesting.

Without 'Tomorrow's Superstar' Rick, critics were writing off The Strawbs as a spent force, and even Cousins considered packing it all in, so he went home to Devon to consider the future. Resorting, as we all do, to a copy of the *I Ching*, the ancient Chinese divination text, he threw the runes in the air and asked the question: Do I continue with The Strawbs or knock it all on the head?

The *I Ching* came up with the following words of wisdom: 'The wanderer has far to go, humble must he constant be, where the paths of wisdom lead, distant is the shadow of the setting sun'. Cousins said: 'This was the book telling me yes, you've got to carry on and do it'. It also gave him the first lyrics written for the album, for a song that is part hymn, part anthem and one that has oblique references to Wakeman's departure. The Strawbs would continue – and, in the process, make what many consider to be their finest and most progressive album, *Grave New World*.

Unlike some of the bands in this book, The Strawbs came from a folk background rather than psychedelic rock or the blues – Cousins and school

pal, Hooper, were influenced by skiffle star Lonnie Donegan, blues legend
Leadbelly, and traditional folk performers such as Ewan MacColl and Peggy
Seeger. Cousins' first instrument was the banjo, and he became one of the
UK's most accomplished players. When Wakeman joined, he helped the band
become more sophisticated in its musical approach, which is why there was
so much consternation when he abruptly left.

His replacement on keyboards, Welshman Blue Weaver, may not have been
as technically gifted as Wakeman, but he was the right person at the right
time, giving the band a heavier, punchier sound (he describes himself as not
a great keyboard player, but a lucky one). Derek John Weaver – called 'Blue'
by his family – came from a more rock background, having been one of the
founders with Andy Fairweather Low of Amen Corner, who had a hit single
with '(If Paradise is) Half as Nice'. Cousins recalls Weaver turning up 'on his
doorstep' after Wakeman left. He said:

> He came in and our whole band (Ford, Hudson, Tony and myself) was
> there. He sat at my piano and we asked, 'What do you play?' and he said, 'I'll
> play some Dave Brubeck'. He played 'Raggedy Waltz' and we thought it was
> very good. So we went to the pub to have a drink. We asked him, 'Do you
> want a beer?' He said, 'Yes, please?' 'Do you like curry?' and he said, 'Yes,
> I like eating curry' and I said, 'OK, you're in the band!' I didn't know if he
> could play our songs. We didn't rehearse; we just said, 'You're in the band'.

'Benedictus' – the song co-written by the *I Ching* – was the first to be
recorded, with Cousins playing electric dulcimer with a Hawaiian slide
through a fuzzbox, while Weaver added organ, piano and Mellotron. The
dulcimer is an early 19th-century fretted instrument with four strings –
although other combinations are known – that is played horizontally, rather
like a Hawaiian guitar. Cousins said Weaver had never played alongside
anything like it before and he found the chords strange (the song is in Bb,
which is unusual for a dulcimer as it is usually tuned to D).

But he seemed to know precisely how the song should go, with a church
organ intro giving it a powerful, hymn-like quality, and the Mellotron swelling
beneath the rousing chorus: 'Bless the daytime, bless the night, bless the
sun which gives us light/Bless the thunder, bless the rain, bless all those
who cause us pain' (Think he's talking about you, there, Wakeman). As the
opener to the new album, it was a defiant statement of intent – The Strawbs
were back, and they didn't need Wakeman to take them into new, uncharted
musical territory. This wasn't folk anymore – this was a new hybrid of genres
that seemed to stretch almost across Time itself.

'Benedictus' was the only song produced by Tony Visconti, recorded at
Island Studios because Island Records were keen to sign The Strawbs but
couldn't come up with the dough. Visconti went on to produce T-Rex, but his
work on the track set the template for the rest of the album and, after that,

the songs were pretty much recorded in the order they eventually appeared. This was partly because Cousins had a theme for the album – it was the story of a man's life from the cradle to the grave, kept deliberately vague to shoehorn the songs in.

So second track, 'Hey Little Man...Thursday's Child', is a father talking to his son, telling him to slow down and spend an hour without care. Think 'Father and Son' by Cat Stevens. You may know from the nursery rhyme that Thursday's Child has 'far to go', which leads nicely on from the wanderer in 'Benedictus' (although in the Scottish version, the child is sad and wise). It's a gentle, solo acoustic number by Cousins that is reprised at the end of side one, but the second version is Wednesday's child, who is 'full of woe' – perhaps older and wiser now.

Track three, 'Queen of Dreams', was written by Cousins and was the most psychedelic, experimental song the band had recorded up to then, opening with backwards acoustic guitar chords, almost fairground organ accompaniment from Weaver and dense harmonies in the verses. Cousins once again plugs his dulcimer through a fuzzbox for a sinuous, Indian-style instrumental and there is a central section of Mellotron sound effects before the song exits on Hudson's frantic drumming.

The lyrics are more typical of psychedelic-cum-progressive fare, with bucolic images of forests, mountains and valleys, inspired by a trip to Rimini in Italy on an earlier tour. Cousins said in the CD liner notes: 'Rimini has a magnificent long white beach with a pine forest, framed by the mountains. In the pine forest, we climbed up to the observation platforms by standing on one another's shoulders – it seemed we were floating on top of the trees'.

The following two tracks – which we'll discuss in reverse order – both drew their inspiration from the same events. As a writer, Cousins was always influenced by what was going on around him, and 1972 was a busy year for dramatic events, particularly if you lived in Northern Ireland. The province suffered its worst year of the Troubles, with more fatalities packed into those twelve months than at any other time in its history of sectarian hatred and violence.

The most infamous massacre was Bloody Sunday, when British soldiers from the First Battalion of the Parachute Regiment killed fourteen innocent, unarmed civilians on a peace march, some shot in the back as they tried to flee to safety, some gunned down as they went to help wounded friends. The youngest victims were just seventeen, the oldest a 59-year-old man who was just passing by on his way to visit a pal.

But Bloody Sunday was just one of many outrages in 1972. In February, the IRA exploded a bomb at an army barracks in Aldershot, killing seven. That was followed by Bloody Friday in July, when IRA bombs across Belfast killed nine people. Just two days before, a car bomb ended the life of the youngest victim of the Troubles, a five-month-old boy.

At the end of July, three car bombs in Claudy, Co Londonderry, claimed nine lives, while three British soldiers were killed when the IRA blew up their armoured personnel carrier near Dungannon. Meanwhile, the infamous Shankill Butchers – a group of brutal loyalists – began kidnapping, torturing and murdering Catholics. By the end of the year, the death toll was 479 people killed, including 130 British soldiers, and 4,876 injured.

That year, Dave Cousins was watching a documentary on the Troubles showing children in Belfast playing at being soldiers, wearing tin hats and carrying toy rifles. They were asked to paint pictures and many depicted soldiers lying dead in the gutters, reflecting the view they had of the horrors going on around them. The programme profoundly affected Cousins, who, while not being particularly religious, was a Catholic and perhaps empathised with the community in Northern Ireland. He said: 'I thought that if this was how they felt about life, the conflict could continue forever – how would it ever end?'

Even today, the song those images inspired, 'New World', throbs with anger and desperation, with its powerful Mellotron opening and simple, folk-like structure. 'There's blood in the dust where the city's heart beats', Cousins sings, 'The children play games that they take from the streets. How can you teach when you've so much to learn?' 50 years on, there is peace of a sort in Northern Ireland, but the divisions and the hatred are still there, played out now in political brinkmanship and deadlock. Will they learn? Not while there's money and votes involved, they won't.

But I digress. What gives the song its power and impact are, firstly, those dramatic opening Mellotron chords – E minor, B minor, Cmaj7, Bsus4, chord fans – and, secondly, Cousins screaming 'May you rot!' at the cowards planning destruction behind the locked door. In a somewhat amateur video shot to accompany the album's release, the message was driven home by showing scenes of Northern Ireland mayhem as Cousins' impassioned vocals ripped the cowards to shreds. And, of course, the title is a play on *Brave New World*, the Aldous Huxley novel about a dystopian future.

A song covering similar ground but with a completely different approach was supplied by John Ford. 'Heavy Disguise' was inspired by the Jethro Tull single, 'A Witch's Promise' – not the lyrical content but the distinctive 6/8 time signature, the rushing strum of the acoustic guitar and swiftly changing chords. Unlike Tull, Ford's lyrics were set in the world of reality, not myth – like Cousins, Ford was inspired by a TV report, this time on a Vietnamese demonstration at the US Embassy, but it was also heavily influenced by the situation in Northern Ireland (it was originally called 'IRA Meeting Blues'). His Fulham landlady played a part – he told The Strange Brew website in 2020: 'She would catch me every morning and lecture me about politics and the IRA situation and all that stuff, and 'Heavy Disguise' was a reflection of that'. He sings about the 'fools pretending to be wise' and how faith is used as a 'heavy disguise', and usually as an excuse for oppressing someone.

The Strawbs tried the song out with the entire band, but it didn't seem to work – something about the swiftly changing chords and the choppy, folkie nature of the acoustic guitar backing suggested it needed something more stately beneath it. So arranger Robert Kirby, who had worked with Nick Drake and later became The Strawbs' second keyboard player, put together a small brass band from the London Symphony Orchestra that plays from about halfway through the song.

For side two, Cousins delved back into his folk roots with 'The Flower and the Young Man', which opens with acapella vocals from the band and features Hooper taking verses. To be honest, it's more folk-rock than prog, but it is lifted by Weaver on harmonium, organ, Clavioline (an early synthesiser bolted onto the side of the piano) and the ever-present Mellotron. Lyrically, we're in the folk world of young men out a-roving and meeting fair maidens, while the seasons change through winter, spring, summer and autumn. The words are, in fact, a reference to a love affair Cousins once had but in a heavy disguise to avoid upsetting his wife.

She was upset enough anyway by the angriest song on the album, the vitriolic 'Tomorrow' – she thought lyrics such as, 'You talked of me with acid tongue, and pointed trembling spiteful hands. Your presence almost overwhelmed' were about her. They weren't; they were about Rick Wakeman, penned in the bitter aftermath of his sudden departure from the band and in response to an interview he had done. At the end, Cousins dismisses him with 'While yesterday, which meant so much, has grown so far away'. So there.

'Tomorrow' offers a fantastic group performance, with Weaver's organ taking centre stage as he races up and down the keyboard, matched by Cousins playing some wailing, crying guitar that at times is almost heavy metal! There's a long instrumental ending in which Cousins and Weaver match each other in dexterity on what is almost a minor-key jig before reprising the opening, crying guitar phrase. What's even more impressive is this was the very first time Cousins had played electric guitar on record.

Side two suffers a little from too many short songs – 'On Growing Older' is one of them, an early composition that channels The Byrds' jingle-jangle guitar and would have fitted better on the Dragonfly album than here. But the theme fitted the concept, with lyrics about looking back on youth and regretting the time that was wasted.

Then there's an oddity, a Hooper song that definitely is a bit of a throwback. 'Ah Me, Ah My' was originally offered up for the band's first album but didn't make it – this time, its theme of reminiscing fitted Cousins' concept. Like 'On Growing Older', it made its first appearance on a 1969 sampler album designed to encourage other artists to cover Cousins and Hooper songs, although it's hard to imagine that anyone would have been much interested in what is a pastiche of a vaudeville number, complete with Old Tyme orchestra scored by Tony Visconti. It is just one minute and 26 seconds long, and all the better for it.

The album ends with two slow songs. The eastern-influenced 'Is it Today, Lord', which opens with sitar and harmonium, is a cross between The Incredible String Band and George Harrison, particularly when Hudson gets on the tablas and the song goes into a sort of 'Within You, Without You' vibe. And, finally, we have a short piano ballad as 'the wanderer, with his heavy load' follows the signpost to 'The Journey's End' – a sad but fitting end to the album, marred only by a rather hurried fadeout.

Grave New World was the most successful Strawbs album so far, with reviewers calling it a 'real work of art' and 'the folk-rock equivalent of Sgt Pepper', and fans responded by sending it to number eleven in the UK charts, selling 100,000 copies in Britain alone. Posterity has been even kinder, acknowledging it as a powerful, majestic (if a little downbeat) album, and opener 'Benedictus' perhaps being the best thing The Strawbs ever recorded.

Sadly, *Grave New World* finished as it started, with a departure. Tony Hooper, who, with Cousins, had founded the band as a folk trio eight years earlier, decided the band was *too* prog and quit. As for The Strawbs, they had their biggest commercial success in 1973 with the thoroughly untypical single 'Part of the Union'. But that led to an acrimonious split, leaving Cousins to almost recreate the band again from scratch.

Clearly, the wanderer still had far to go...

Focus – *Focus 3*

Personnel:
Thijs van Leer: vocals, Hammond organ, piano, alto flute, piccolo, harpsichord
Jan Akkerman: guitars, lute
Bert Ruiter: bass guitar
Pierre van der Linden: drums
Recorded July 1972 at Olympic Studios, London
Produced by Mike Vernon
Engineered by George Chkiantz
Label: Imperial Records
Release date: November 1972
Chart: places: UK 6, Netherlands 1, Norway 20, US 35, Australia 36
Tracks: 'Round Goes the Gossip' (Thijs van Leer), 'Love Remembered' (Jan
Akkerman), 'Sylvia' (Van Leer), 'Carnival Fugue' (Van Leer), 'Focus III' (Van Leer),
'Answers? Questions! Questions? Answers!' (Akkerman, Bert Ruiter), 'Anonymous
II Part 1' (Van Leer, Akkerman, Ruiter, Pierre van der Linden), 'Anonymous II
Part 2' (Van Leer, Akkerman, Ruiter, Van der Linden), 'Elspeth of Nottingham'
(Akkerman), 'House of the King' (Akkerman).

The story so far...

The band was formed in 1969 by keyboard player, flautist and singer Thijs
van Leer, who recruited Martijn Dresden on bass and Hans Cleuver on
drums after meeting them at radio sessions in Hilversum, Netherlands.
Van Leer, born in Amsterdam, had studied music at university, released
solo singles and was part of a theatre cabaret act when Jan Akkerman
was invited to join the trio. Akkerman, also from Amsterdam, had been in
various bands, including Brainbox, with his friend, Pierre van der Linden.
They became the pit band for the Dutch touring production of the hippie
musical *Hair* (and are on a cast album recorded in 1970) while building
a reputation as a live band. During time off from *Hair*, Focus recorded
their first album in London, funded by Dutch record producer Hubert
Terheggan, but couldn't find anyone willing to release it. The band then
recorded 'House of the King', written by Akkerman, which secured them
a deal with Imperial Records. Their debut album, *Focus Plays Focus* (later
retitled *In and Out of Focus*), was released in September 1970, and 'House
of the King' reached number ten in the Dutch charts. Akkerman, unhappy
with Dresden and Cleuver, threatened to quit unless they were sacked. After
intense negotiations, Cleuver was replaced by Brainbox pal van der Linden,
also from Amsterdam, and Dresden replaced by Cyril Havermans. The new
line-up recorded *Focus II* (better known as *Moving Waves*), which was an
international hit in 1971, along with the single 'Hocus Pocus'. Havermans
quit because he wanted to do more singing and was replaced by Bert Ruiter
from Hilversum, who played in various local bands and once auditioned
alongside van der Linden.

The album

It just came out of the blue. There was Jan Akkerman, playing the thunderous, driving riff, there was Pierre van der Linden filling in a few bars with his powerful drums and then it was Thijs van Leer's turn. Suddenly, from out of nowhere, came the yodel. 'It was just there during rehearsal. I never yodelled before', he said. 'It just came out of the sky. And there it was, in that song'.

The song was 'Hocus Pocus', the place a castle outside Amsterdam, and the band was Focus who, in 1972, released two singles containing yodelling that reached the charts of several European countries. In the UK, both 'Hocus Pocus' and follow-up 'Sylvia' were in the UK Top 40 at the same time! With yodelling! It has never happened before and will likely never happen again.

But we shouldn't focus – pun intended – on the yodelling alone. There was falsetto screaming as well, again from van Leer that came about because his instruments – organ and flute – were the softies in the band compared to Akkerman's guitar, van der Linden's drums and Ruiter's bass. With those three at full pelt, the only way van Leer could compete was with his voice – and with primal sounds, not words.

Once again, let's not focus – pun intended again – on the vocals alone. Focus had (and still have at the time of writing) tremendous musical chops and the ability to write hard-rocking songs, 20-minute prog monsters and delicate instrumental ballads, all with catchy melodic hooks that have lasted 50 years. There are a number of contenders for 'greatest Dutch Prog Band Ever', but I nominate Focus. Let's just give them the award and be done with it.

As you can see from a quick perusal of the story so far, it wasn't all plain sailing. In less than three short years – more like two, really – they had managed to lose no fewer than three members and plant the seeds for an animosity between van Leer and Akkerman that seems to have persisted to the present day (when asked to contribute his memories to this book, Mr Akkerman replied: 'I'm temporarily out of Focus...'). Between 1969 and 1971 both Akkerman and van der Linden threatened to quit for various reasons. Then there was the time an earlier incarnation of the band ended up in jail after trashing the dressing room at a music contest in Majorca.

But we shouldn't focus – there's that pun again – on the trials and tribulations because, sometimes, out of adversity comes great art. Van Leer claims Akkerman was inspired to write their breakthrough instrumental hit 'House of the King' by van Leer's flute improvisations during the ill-fated gig in Majorca (although Akkerman claims he wrote it on a mountain with a beautiful Spanish stewardess). That single led to a recording career that has spanned five decades – their most recent album, *Focus 11*, was released in 2019, and they are still touring, playing in Maastricht in the Netherlands as I write this sentence!

When they went into the studio in July 1972 to record their third album, it was with their most stable line-up so far. I mean, no one had quit or threatened to quit in the last ten months. They had just completed their first

UK tour, made their UK TV debut on *The Old Grey Whistle Test* and been voted 'Brightest Hope' by *Melody Maker* and 'Best New Talent' by the *New Musical Express.*

Initially, the plan was to make a single album, a follow-up to *Moving Waves,* which had hit the Top 10 in the US, UK, Netherlands and Canada. But it had been over a year since they had made that album, so they had so much material, both individually and together, that the decision was made to make their third release a double. In the event, they *didn't* have enough material and the 1970 recording of 'House of the King', with Dresden and Cleuver both uncredited, was tacked on the end of side four.

'Hocus Pocus' had been created out of a jam session, but Focus didn't usually work in that way – certainly not van Leer, anyway. He liked to carefully craft his compositions before presenting them to the rest of the band. For example, the absolutely brilliant 'Sylvia' – track three on the album – dates back to 1968 and was originally written as a cabaret song for Sylvia Alberts, a member of the theatre group van Leer was in, and originally titled 'I Thought I Could Do Everything on My Own, I Was Always Stripping the Town Alone'. She turned it down, so van Leer used her name as the title when the composition was taken out, brushed off and recorded by the band.

Like 'Hocus Pocus', 'Sylvia' encapsulates practically everything that made Focus unique back in the early Seventies. Akkerman's muscular chords, played high up the neck of the guitar? Check. Lyrical guitar melody set to descending bass line? Check. Impromptu yodelling and screaming, along with swelling Hammond organ chords? Check. Frequent surprise key changes? Check. A False ending, leading into a restatement of the opening chords (F, C, G, Eb, Ab, Eb, Bb, written by van Leer's brother Frank) while Akkerman improvises over the top? Check. The only thing missing is van Leer's flute but, apart from that, this is Focus distilled into three and a half exciting, breathless minutes.

Opening track, 'Round Goes the Gossip', also composed by van Leer, is in a similar vein, although with many more twists and turns in the melody and chords (and it will take a better musician than I to fathom them out). The song comes from a very lofty inspiration, the works of first-century BCE Roman poet Publius Vergilius Maro, otherwise known as Virgil. In the Aeneid, his epic poem about the Trojan Aeneas who fled the fall of Troy and founded Rome, Virgil shows how destructive gossip can be by creating a character called Rumour, who spreads malicious lies through the Heavens and the Earth.

In the song, van Leer repeats the title over frenetic drumming from van der Linden and slicing chords and little riffs from Akkerman, before there is a sudden stop and, over gentle Hammond organ, he recites Latin verses from the Aeneid – 'Extemplo libyae magnas it fama per urbes, Fama, malum qua non aliud velocius ullum, Mobilitate viget virisque adquirit eundo'. There are a few lines more in this vein, and it translates roughly as, 'Immediately the great news of Libya spread through the cities, Fame, an evil which no other hastened. He thrives on mobility and acquires strength by walking'.

When the song proper returns, there's something of an organ/guitar duel going on over a fast, jazzy rhythm before we get a restatement of the initial 'Round Goes the Gossip' theme, fading out on a key change that keeps going up and up, with van Leer practically screeching over the top. As an opener, it's a thoroughly baffling piece of music full of energy, wit and unpredictable musical changes.

Akkerman provides the second track, 'Love Remembered', a touching instrumental melody played on flute over the guitarist's acoustic finger-picking, inspired by the idea of lovers on a country walk. This being Focus, there are additional swoops of sound in the background, and everything picks up a bit when drums, bass and organ come in. But it is essentially the delicate, lyrical side of the band, something Akkerman frequently provided because of his love of Renaissance music and his proficiency on all kinds of stringed instruments.

Track four, 'Carnival Fugue', is a van Leer composition, borrowing rather heavily from Johann Sebastian Bach's 'The Well-Tempered Clavier', a set of preludes and fugues in all 24 major and minor keys, written as practice pieces for keyboard players. 'Clavier' meant any keyboards in Bach's day, mostly harpsichord and clavichord, but most modern interpretations are played on piano.

Van Leer's tune opens with variations on four well-tempered piano chords – Ab major seventh, G minor, F major and C major – played in a slow, stately fashion with almost indistinct guitar twiddling underneath from Akkerman. There's a sad wistfulness about it all, alleviated somewhat by those definite, optimistic major chords. After a minute and a half, van Leer moves into a faster Bachian tune in a minor key, the rest of the band enter and the tune suddenly becomes a jazz number, led by van Leer's cascading improvisations. After that, he takes over on piccolo and organ with something that sounds almost calypso, Akkerman improvising on guitar over three repetitive chords before fading out. It is an unusual piece full of different moods and ideas but, somehow, still manages to hang together as a single composition.

The original side two opens with another van Leer tune, 'Focus III'. It had become a thing for the band to include a track named after itself on practically every studio album (there isn't one on *Hamburger Concerto* or *Focus Con Proby*) and we are currently up to 'Focus 11'. They are frequently some of the most memorable, melodic moments on the albums and 'Focus III' is no exception. Opening with moody organ arpeggios, it eventually gives Akkerman the opportunity to play an uplifting, melodic guitar solo before heading back into moody territory. This combination of dark and light, in which the guitar feels controlled and restrained before bursting out joyfully, gives this piece a sense of orchestral drama.

'Focus III' moves directly into a Ruiter/Akkerman composition, 'Answers? Questions! Questions? Answers!'. Ruiter came up with the menacing bass riff that opens proceedings, doubled up on guitar with van Leer offering dramatic organ washes. Akkerman speeds things up with some fast riffing before allowing van Leer to improvise on organ. We go back to the bass riff before Akkerman lets loose with fast guitar riffs again and a lengthy improv section over shifting organ keys. Akkerman is all over this track and his playing is aggressive and dominating – but there are also times when he delivers beautiful, lyrical guitar phrases over complementary organ playing.

Things slow down for a pretty flute solo in a minor key that builds in intensity before Akkerman lets rip again, finally coming to a close after nearly fourteen minutes with the repeat of the minor chords that played under van Leer's flute. And so ends a magnificent piece of half-composed, half-improvised Focus music with, to my ears, the only misstep being Akkerman's harsh guitar flourish at the end.

On the original vinyl, the longest track Focus ever recorded, the 27-minute 'Anonymous II', took up side three of the double LP. How did they fit 27 minutes on one side of vinyl, you may ask, and the answer is they didn't – the final seven and a half minutes were placed at the start of side four. Thanks to CDs and digital streaming, we can listen to the track as it was no doubt intended: as one long, glorious piece of music. But in order to give the listener a short respite, the CD version placed 'Elspeth of Nottingham' between the two long tracks. As we are in analogue 1972, we'll stick to the vinyl running order.

There was an 'Anonymous' on the band's debut album that was part Tudor fanfare, part Jethro Tull flute improv and part guitar, bass and drums workout, ending in a restatement of the Tudor theme on flute. Version two opens with exactly the same theme, this time played on organ and guitar at about twice the speed. A slightly discordant flute does the breathless Tull thing over pounding drums, followed by a lengthy organ solo over the single chord of G minor.

At the six-and-a-half-minute mark, the tune comes to an apparent halt, before Ruiter's tentative bass probes gently through the silence, gradually developing a riffy improvisation that encourages van der Linden and Akkerman to join in with a funky rhythm, leading to a lengthy guitar workout over the single chord of D minor. After eighteen minutes, van der Linden gets a drum solo before the track ends on the restatement of the Tudor theme.

Conceived as an opportunity for every band member to get a solo spot, and probably better experienced live than on vinyl, 'Anonymous II' is a little too basic to really work as a 27-minute epic – it lacks the variety of moods and tempos the likes of Yes, Jethro Tull and Genesis put into their side-long tracks. But it is packed full of great improvisations by musicians at the top of their game.

The new tracks end with 'Elspeth of Nottingham', penned by Akkerman after a trip to the Cotswolds in England in 1967, during which he saw classical guitarist, Julian Bream, play the lute. Conjuring up aural visions of mediaeval England, Akkerman plucks the lute with van Leer playing what sounds like a recorder, with a backdrop of birdsong and occasional mooing cows. The UK version of the album then rounds off with the 1970 recording of 'House of the King', which was subsequently left off the CD releases.

Focus 3 didn't quite repeat the success of 1971's *Moving Waves* but still topped the chart in the Netherlands and reached the UK top ten – in fact, both albums were in the UK charts at the same time thanks to the popularity of 'Sylvia'. In the US, *Focus 3* reached number 89 but appeared to sell steadily, shifting half a million copies there by 1973.

At the time, *Down Beat* magazine called it 'a sincere, emotional mixture of classical, jazz, and rock'; a retrospective review for *Allmusic* says, 'To be frank, this LP has it all: diverse songs, astounding musicianship, one of the finest singles ever released – *Focus III* should unquestionably be ranked alongside the likes of *Revolver*, *Dark Side of the Moon*, and any others of rock's greatest'. Most Focus fans would probably agree that it would have been even more successful as a single LP, shorn of 'House of the King' and a good chunk of 'Anonymous II'.

As it is, *Focus 3* is a flawed but essential classic from a band that, 50 years on, is still making its own brand of idiosyncratic Dutch prog.

Santana – *Caravanserai*

Personnel:
Carlos Santana: guitars, vocals, percussion
Neal Schon: guitar
Gregg Rolie: organ, electric piano, vocals, piano
Douglas Rauch: bass, guitar
Douglas Rodrigues: guitar
Wendy Haas: piano
Tom Rutley: acoustic bass
Michael Shrieve: drums, percussion, vocals
José 'Chepito' Areas: percussion, congas, timbales, bongos
James Mingo Lewis: percussion, congas, bongos, vocals, acoustic piano
Armando Peraza: percussion, bongos
Hadley Caliman: saxophone, flute
Rico Reyes: vocals
Lenny White: castanets
Tom Coster: electric piano
Recorded 21 February to 5 May 1972 at Columbia Studios, San Francisco
Produced by Carlos Santana and Michael Shrieve
Recorded & engineered by Glen Kolotkin & Mike Larner
Label: Columbia/CBS
Release date: 11 October 1972
Chart places: US: 8, Germany: 41
Tracks: 'Eternal Waves of Reincarnation' (Tom Rutley, Neal Schon, Michael Shrieve), 'Waves Within' (Doug Rauch, Gregg Rolie, Carlos Santana), 'Look Up (To See What's Coming Down)' (Rauch, Rolie, Santana), 'Just in Time to See the Sun' (Rolie, Santana, Shrieve), 'Song of the Wind' (Rolie, Santana, Schon), 'All the Love of the Universe' (Santana, Schon), 'Future Primitive' (Jose Areas, Mingo Lewis), 'Stone Flower' (Music: Antonio Carlos Jobim, Lyrics: Santana, Shrieve), 'La Fuente De Ritmo (Lewis), 'Every Step of the Way' (Shrieve)

The story so far...

Carlos Santana left his hometown of Autlan, Mexico, for Tijuana and then San Francisco, first playing violin like his father and then electric guitar. In 1966 he formed the Santana Blues Band, later shortened to Santana, to play at the Fillmore West in San Fran. By 1969 the band consisted of Santana on guitar, Gregg Rolie on organ and vocals, Michael Carabello on percussion, David Brown on bass, Michael Shrieve on drums and Jose Areas on percussion. In 1968 the band got a record deal with Columbia and released their debut eponymous album in 1969, shortly after a triumphant appearance at the Woodstock Festival shot them to international fame. *Santana* reached number four in the US, number 26 in the UK, and a single, 'Evil Ways', was a Top Ten US hit. The second album, *Abraxas*, in 1970, was number one in the US and Australia, number two in Canada, number three in Norway, number seven in the UK, France and the Netherlands. Single 'Black Magic Woman' was a Top Ten hit in the US and Canada. *Santana III*, released in 1971, was another chart-topper that marked the addition of guitarist Neal Schon. But internal divisions were about to tear the classic line-up apart ...

The album

Sex and drugs and rock 'n' roll – according to Ian Dury, they can be very good indeed. But sometimes, they can be not so good. For Santana, the Latin rock band that shot to fame thanks to a mind-blowing, energy-packed performance at Woodstock and, in 1972, released arguably their most prog album, they were poison. In his autobiography, *The Universal Tone: Bringing My Story to Light*, Carlos Santana said:

> The rock 'n' roll lifestyle was taking over; it wasn't just the women or the cars or the cocaine and other excesses, it was also the attitude. We used to say that we were from the streets and we were real – we'd look at other bands that were making it and judge how they acted. 'We're never going to be assholes like that', we'd say. But I saw how some people in the band were acting, and I was thinking to myself, 'It's easy to see why a lot of bands fail – they OD on themselves'.

In other words, Santana were turning into assholes. Perhaps it was inevitable – the band's meteoric rise from a little San Fran blues quartet to a sprawling, Latin/rock fusion behemoth was enough to make even the most level-headed of artists go off the rails (except Carlos, of course). It was only a few years before that the hitherto virtually unknown Santana had become the stars of Woodstock – and only a few years prior to that when Carlos himself was washing dishes at a drive-in restaurant to meet the payments on his new guitar.

Success, however, had gone to their heads (but not to Carlos's, of course) and various members of the band started pulling in different musical directions. Rolie and some of the others wanted to emphasise the commercial hard rock elements, while Carlos was immersing himself in spiritual jazz, listening to Miles Davis, John Coltrane and Pharoah Sanders. He was looking for new ideas and new sounds – becoming more progressive, if you like – while some of the others simply wanted the commercial gravy train to continue thundering down the tracks.

Other pressures weighed down on the band at this time. Percussionist Jose Areas suffered a near-fatal brain haemorrhage, and the band split into those who, like Carlos, wanted to carry on with a replacement and those who felt it was disrespectful, that they should wait until Areas recovered.

With success came money and, inevitably, drugs – particularly heroin, which got its claws into some of the band in 1970 and refused to let go. Carlos liked a bit of weed and even tried heroin a couple of times but decided very early on it wasn't for him – it made him feel like everything he played on guitar was wonderful but when he listened to the recordings, man, what a racket. Heroin told you lies.

By the end of 1970, the drugs were affecting the music. Carlos said: 'There were more fights and arguments than making music – the joy of it felt like it was leaving'.

He decided to take more control of the band, and one of his first moves was to fire bassist David Brown, whose drug use was making him unreliable to a point where he had to serve at least one jail sentence. He was replaced by Tom Rutley, who played upright acoustic bass and took the band further into a jazzy direction. He appeared on a few tracks on *Caravanserai* before returning to his jazz world and was replaced by Doug Rauch. But that wasn't enough to turn the band around. Carlos said:

Many things were still wrong – the drugs and lowlifes and hang-arounders were still getting in the way of the music. It had gotten to the point where people would wake up in the morning still drunk and fucked up from the night before, still totally buzzed on cocaine. Then they'd do more cocaine to wake up, so then they'd be tired and wired, and I was the one who kept putting my foot down. 'They' were mainly [manager] Stan Marcum and Carabello.

Carlos laid down an ultimatum – either Marcum and Carabello went, or he would. Amazingly, the band called his bluff, heading off on tour without the man whose surname was on the concert tickets and marquee signs. But they faced a backlash from the audience, who screamed and booed and demanded to see and hear the guitar wizard himself. After three weeks, Neal Schon called Carlos and told him they wanted him back – and they would send Marcum and Carabello home, replacing the latter with new congo player, James Mingo Lewis. It didn't heal the wounds at first – Carlos said half the band members and crew wanted to beat him up because they felt he was 'killing a good thing'. But the music was getting looser, jazzier and more adventurous. Then Santana went to Peru.

In 1971, Peru was ruled by a military dictatorship headed by General Juan Francisco Velasco Alvarado, who had taken power in a coup some three years before. While not the worst dictator in the world – he actually wanted to help the poor, which is better than some so-called advanced democratic societies that prefer tax breaks for the rich – his rule saw a rise in nationalism and anti-American sentiment. So when Santana arrived at a crowded Lima airport – and were greeted by the twins who booked them with a huge jar of cocaine – there were many locals who were not very happy they were there, particularly communist students who decided to set fire to the venue.

Then, while visiting churches in the city, Carlos and some other members of the band were suddenly arrested and detained by police – for their

109

own safety, they were told. Apparently, the students were becoming more threatening and the musicians were in danger. The gig was abandoned and the band shepherded out of the country on the next available flight to Los Angeles. One of the crew had to cut his hair and shave his moustache to disguise himself so he could get back to the hotel and retrieve the gear.

By the time Santana went back into the studio in March 1972, the internal conflict had turned into sadness. Marcum, Carabello and Brown were gone, while Rolie and Schon had decided to leave after the fourth album to start the band Journey. A heartbroken Carlos found himself turning more and more to Shrieve for musical support – both shared a desire to introduce more jazzy, experimental elements into the music.

Carlos's estrangement from some of his colleagues wasn't just musical – he was delving deeper into Eastern philosophy, particularly the 'wisdom' of fellow guitarist John McLaughlin's guru, Sri Chimnoy. The guru gave McLaughlin the name Mahavishnu and later dubbed Carlos 'Devadip', meaning 'the lamp, light and eye of God'. Carlos wanted to put the philosophies he had absorbed into the music, which further alienated those band members who preferred to plough a more mainstream rock furrow. Having said that, some of the more way-out tracks on *Caravanserai* were co-written by people such as Rolie and Schon, so they clearly weren't averse to experimental music.

The recording sessions showed how fragmented the band had become. Frequently, small groups of people would work separately in the studio before presenting the basic tracks to Carlos, saying, 'we want a guitar solo here'. As a co-composer, he is credited on just six of the ten tracks. But he still managed to create an album in his own image, one that explored all his musical and philosophical interests.

Take the title, *Caravanserai*. That came from the writings of Paramahansa Yogananda, an Indian monk who helped popularise yoga and meditation from the 1920s onwards and was dubbed the 20th century's first superstar guru. It was a place where you could find inner peace, like a philosophical spa. The title of the first track, 'Eternal Caravan of Reincarnation', came from the same source.

Carlos had wanted the album to start with sounds of nature, so engineer Glen Kolotkin recorded a cricket chorus in his own backyard. In comes a rushing fog of sax, played by one of the many guests on the album, Hadley Caliman from Oklahoma. Then Rutley starts a stately, repetitive bass figure and special guest Wendy Haas provides random, echoing piano chords. Shrieve joins with a steady, understated beat while Schon plays gentle jazz guitar chords – Carlos doesn't play guitar on this track at all. It bears some resemblance to Pharoah Sanders' 'Astral Travelling' from his 1971 album *Thembi*, particularly in the repetitive bassline and washes of sound.

Many of the tracks segue into another – Carlos wanted the album to be one long, complete experience. So 'Eternal Caravan of Reincarnation' merges into 'Waves Within', an instrumental clearly inspired by the Mahavishnu Orchestra with its busy bass and horn-like guitar phrases over a repetitive three-chord motif, all laid over busy Latin jazz percussion. It has that feeling of stature, of weight, that McLaughlin could create with his band, with guitar breaks that eschew the blues to create sonic walls of sound. Santana's piercing tone seems to drip with passion, fading out on a long, sustained note.

It mixes into the third instrumental on the album, 'Look Up (To See What's Coming Down)', an upbeat, funky number that could have so easily had some vocals attached to it. Instead, the emphasis is on swelling Hammond organ, driving percussion, bouncing bass, wah-wah-ed guitar chords and occasional lead guitar playing simple, melodic phrases. This segues into 'Just in Time to See the Sun', which appears to repeat some elements of the 'Waves Within' chord progression under Rolie's vocals. Here, we hear elements of the AOR that Rolie would explore more fully with Journey – what lifts this track from the land of the bland is, once again, the busy percussion and Carlos's screaming guitar licks.

Another segue takes us into 'Song of the Wind', one of those trademark instrumentals that are so Santana – his expressive guitar whispering and screaming over a restrained Latin rhythm and washes of organ chords. It's the 'Samba Pa Ti' of the album when Carlos shows he's not only a master of his instrument but has an uncanny ability to transform his bluesy licks into bittersweet melodies.

'Song of the Wind' practically disappears from earshot before the final track on side one, 'All The Love of the Universe', bursts into view with some more Mahavishnu-like chords and repetitive arpeggios, as Rutley's acoustic bass steps up and down under wordless vocals. It then turns into a more straightforward, low-key rock song, with harmony vocals from three or four of the musicians (including Carlos). The catchy chorus of 'Everybody needs a helping hand' is sung over the descending chords of C, E minor and A minor before guitars and organ take turns to improvise over a lengthy outro over frantic percussion, before ending on more Mahavishnu arpeggios.

Side Two is shorter, with just four songs, opening with some assorted percussion and keyboard sounds over an almost indistinct drone. 'Future Primitive' was written by percussionists Areas and Mingo Lewis, so it turns into a showcase for their lightning-fast work on congas, timbales and bongos.

This is followed by a surprising collaboration between Santana and Antonio Carlos Jobim, the Brazilian composer and musician best known for his bossa nova classic, 'The Girl From Ipanema'. He composed the tune, 'Stone Flower', for his 1970 album of the same name – it's an Indian lichen used as a spice. It was Shrieve's idea to write lyrics inspired by the title – 'What's that sound I hear coming from the ground/That' going 'round and 'round I can feel it pull me down/On my knees tears of joy have come to me/As the flower sounds made it plain to see'.

Jobim's original is a medium-paced jazz bossa nova performed on drums played with brushes, acoustic bass, piano and violin, washed with gentle orchestral accompaniment and occasional stabs of brass. Santana ups the emotional and musical content somewhat, although taking it at the same loping speed. Organ, bass and percussion warm up together for a minute before Carlos's guitar comes in over stabs of chords. Then Carlos and Shrieve sing in unison on the verses, punctuated by lead guitar, occasional solo percussion, Rolie's organ licks and Rutley's busy, bouncing bass.

Track nine, 'La Fuente Del Ritmo', is about as Latin Santana as you can get – massed, driving percussion with Carlo's commanding guitar playing spikey riffs, sometimes in perfect harmony with Schon, fast electric piano from new recruit Coster, and Rutley's repetitive acoustic bass anchoring everything together. There is no tune as such – it's more of a frantic Latin workout that fades out after four and a half minutes. This is one of just two appearances on the album of Armando Peraza, a Cuban percussionist who worked with such greats as Dizzy Gillespie, Dexter Gordon and Charles Mingus.

Finally, the album ends on the nine-minute 'Every Step of the Way'. Like some of the other tracks on the album, it has a fairly long introduction of drums, bass and organ, all ploughing along together in the single chord of A. There's some angular, atonal guitar before it crashes into a louder, faster instrumental with a repetitive five-note motif over alternating chords of A minor and G minor. Caliman pops in with breathy, growly flute improvisations, then the guitarists really cut loose as an orchestra swells up beneath. I say 'guitarists' because it is not clear who plays what here – the sleeve notes credit both Schon and Carlos on this track. If Schon is indeed playing much of the lead, then he is doing an absolutely flawless Carlos impersonation.

'Every Step of the Way' was Carlos's favourite track on the album – he said: 'For two reasons... first because it sounds like what we really loved back then: Herbie Hancock's *Crossings*. The song also reminds me of Shrieve because he wrote it and because of how we played together'.

And that's *Caravanserai*, which really has to be taken as a whole body of work, from the crickets chirping away at the opening to the cacophonous rave-up at the end. Sure, there are some moments that show the pull various members were exerting to drag the band towards a more commercial sound. But every time they do that, it snaps back into something more spiritual and interesting – and definitely more prog.

Sadly, the album divided everyone back in 1972 and still does today. Schon said it wasn't really Santana any more, and Rolie later told *The Music Aficionado* in 2018:

I liked the exploration on the album *Caravanserai*, but I didn't want to make it a mainstay of what we did. I also didn't want to lose the relationship we had developed with our audience. I couldn't see throwing that away for this new musical direction. So like most bands, we fell apart. But when I look at it now, I realise that if we hadn't been the people we were at that time, that music probably would never have happened. So it's okay.

Even the record label had its qualms, with Columbia/CBS boss, Clive Davis, telling Carlos there was 'not one single within a thousand miles of this album'. Why would you want to do this? he asked. When he heard the title was *Caravanserai*, he added: 'More like career suicide'. It wasn't, but with no hit singles like 'Oye Coma Va' or 'Evil Ways' to play on the radio, sales of *Caravanserai* were not as good as Santana's first three albums. Reviews were mixed, with a positive reaction from *Melody Maker*, and *Rolling Stone* saying it spoke to 'the universality of Man'. But other critics responded with collective bafflement (always a sign of a good prog album, in my view).

Posterity has recognised that Santana the musician was striving for greater things with *Caravanserai*. It's an album that has to be taken as a whole, with two sides of almost continuous music weaving through jazz, rock, funk and bossa nova. Some fans find it disappointing when set against the band's more accessible output, and Carlos himself took the band back to its more commercial roots with the 1976 release, *Amigos*.

Website *Allmusic* is right when it says the album 'requires a number of listenings in order to be absorbed and fully appreciated. But make no mistake: this is one of Santana's finest accomplishments'.

Curved Air – *Phantasmagoria*

Personnel:
Sonja Kristina: lead vocals, acoustic guitar
Francis Monkman: keyboards, electric guitar, percussion
Florian Pilkington-Miksa: drums
Darryl Way: violin, keyboards, tubular bells, melon
Mike Wedgwood: bass, backing vocals, guitars, percussion
Recorded March 1972 at Advision Studios and EMS, both in London
Produced by Curved Air and Colin Caldwell
Label: Warner Bros
Release date: April 1972
Chart places: UK: 20
Tracks: 'Marie Antoinette' (Darryl Way, Sonja Kristina Linwood), 'Melinda (More Or Less)' (Linwood), 'Not Quite the Same' (Way, Linwood), 'Cheetah' (Way), 'Ultra-Vivaldi' (Way, Francis Monkman), 'Phantasmagoria' (Monkman), 'Whose Shoulder Are You Looking Over Anyway?' (Monkman), 'Over and Above' (Monkman), 'Once a Ghost, Always a Ghost' (Monkman, Linwood)

The story so far...

In 1969, Francis Monkman, from Hampstead, North London, met Darryl Way, of Taunton, Somerset, in a music shop where the latter had experimentally amplified his violin. They invited pianist Nick Simon, bassist Rob Martin and drummer Florian Pilkington-Miksa (Paddington, London), to form a group inspired by US psychedelic rock band Spirit. Sisyphus, as the new collective was called, provided musical accompaniment for a play at a London theatre and impressed Mark Hanau, who offered to manage them. He brought in folk singer Sonja Kristina from Brentwood, Essex. Simon left and the band became Curved Air, named after an album by minimalist composer Terry Riley. Following a successful UK tour, the band was signed by Warner Bros as the US company's first UK band and their debut album, *Air Conditioning,* was released in November 1970, reaching number eight in the UK charts. Martin left after suffering a hand injury and was replaced by Ian Eyre, who played on Curved Air's most successful single, 'Back Street Luv', and second album – entitled, imaginatively, *Second Album* – both in 1971. But by the time they came to record their third album, serious musical differences were emerging ...

The album

If you looked closely at the records, you could almost see the split coming. On both *Second Album* and *Phantasmagoria,* the first sides are dominated by Darryl Way and the second by Francis Monkman. Monkman was the experimental one – he loved the music of Terry Riley and suggested the band name, taken from Riley's *A Rainbow in Curved Air.* He liked creating sounds that had never been heard before and loved jamming – real, deep, cosmic jamming – just to see what would come out of it.

But Way was the opposite. On stage, he could be a flamboyant showman, with a scarf swinging from the end of his violin and explosions going off but, in the studio, he was a precise perfectionist who liked everything worked out in advance and was more interested in crafting short, catchy songs. Way co-wrote the UK number four hit, 'Back Street Luv'; Monkman, the thirteen-minute prog beast on *Second Album*, 'Piece of Mind. The two respected each other but never saw eye-to-eye. By the time the tour for the third album, *Phantasmagoria*, was over, so were Curved Air - briefly.

As with many bands at the time, the constant gigging demanded by management took a serious toll on the members' health. In late 1971, drummer Pilkingon-Miksa fell ill and was replaced by Barry DeSouza for a few months. Then bassist Ian Eyre collapsed in Hollywood, his vegetarian lifestyle corrupted by overwork and Valium. He was replaced by Derby-born Mike Wedgwood from the band Arthur's Mother and it was this line-up that went into the studio to record the third album.

One of the first things the band did was to update some of its equipment, bringing in a VCS3 synthesiser. The instrument was invented a few years earlier by the Electronic Music Studios company, formed by boffins, Peter Zinovieff, Tristram Cary and David Cockerall. It was the first truly portable synth, housed in a small wooden box, but it had notoriously unreliable tuning. Despite that, it was popular with progressive rock bands – Curved Air borrowed one for previous album *Air Conditioning*, and Monkman was agitating for the band to get its own. In the liner notes for *Phantasmagoria*'s 2018 release, Kristina said:

At this point in our career, Francis was reaching out to the stratosphere when it came to creative ideas. So that's why we used synthesisers this time round ... Francis is an engineering buff himself and once built an analogue computer by himself. So he was really fascinated by the work going on in this area and how it might be used to push music forward.

Monkman was also the most prolific writer in the band and an accomplished arranger who could take other members' ideas and make them so much better. This no doubt contributed towards a certain amount of friction with Way, who also felt the band had gone as far as it could experimentally and needed to concentrate on being more commercial. However, this clash didn't seem to develop into open warfare – Monkman and Way managed to produce the album together and, by all accounts, the recording was an enjoyable, stress-free affair.

But the finished product certainly reflects the schizophrenic nature of the band. Actually, there are three personalities at work here: experimental Monkman, commercial Way and storytelling Kristina, whose work owes as much to folk music as it does to prog.

In fact, she sang her solo composition, 'Melinda (More or Less)', when she auditioned for the band, but they thought it was too folky to record. Monkman rearranged it to add violin, harpsichord and flute to Kristina's finger-picked acoustic guitar – the only time she plays an instrument on the album – and the song takes on a more wistful, mysterious air without betraying its obvious folk roots.

Kristina also contributed lyrics to two of Way's melodies; the powerful album opener, 'Marie Antoinette' and the quirky and humorous, 'Not Quite the Same'. Kristina always wanted to write about Marie Antoinette Josephe Jeanne, wife of French king Louis XVI, who both lost their heads when the monarchy was abolished at the end of the 18th century (and she probably *didn't* say 'Let them eat cake'). The lyrics seem to place her firmly on the side of the revolutionaries chanting 'Vive la nation!', while the music moves from a dreamy, lyrical opening to a heavy rock workout, with the sound of a guillotine hacking off a head – actually Way chopping through a melon with a knife. 'Not Quite the Same' contains no fewer than four trumpets and four trombones (Way knew the players from his time at the Royal College of Music) for a saucy tale about, ahem, a lonely man's self-abuse, set to a bouncing 6/8 rhythm.

Way's other contributions include 'Cheetah', a powerful instrumental featuring his lightning-fast violin over harpsichord, guitars and drums, ending with a cheetah's roar (the band named the sound effect Doris and credited it on the album). He also gets a credit on the short but sweet 'Ultra-Vivaldi'. That's because he wrote the original tune for *Air Conditioning* before Monkman reproduced it on a Synthi 100, another EMS product that was made out of three VSC 3s and possessed two duo phonic keyboards, so four voices could be played at once. The track gets faster and faster before disappearing up its own inputs.

Side two is dominated by four Monkman compositions that really make up a four-part suite, one of them with lyrics by Kristina. The first part is 'Phantasmagoria', which gave its name to the album. The word refers to a form of horror theatre using slides and lanterns that became popular in the 19th century and was also the title of a humorous poem by Alice in Wonderland author Lewis Carroll, about an annoying ghost haunting a new house. Monkman reworks it as a plea to the house's owner not to be scared but to treat the ghost as a friend, adding lines from the original poem. Monkman fashions a fast-moving, seemingly ever-changing melody that winds its way over hurried, scurrying backing from the band.

A line from part one – 'keep looking over your shoulder' – inspires the title of part two, a short experiment in electronic sound effects recorded at the EMS studios. The robotic voices were the first known use of a vocoder effect on a commercially-released rock track – Kristina's spoken words (the Lewis Carroll poem and the line from part one) were put through the synthesiser and output as watery, robotic noises.

After a good three and a half minutes of assorted sounds, we segue into the best track on the album, the thunderous 'Over and Above', in which Way and Monkman duel on violin and synthesiser over a massed backing of organ, electric piano, guitar, tubular bells, gong, drums, xylophone, vibes, trumpets and trombones. Phew! Kristina sings lyrics about being a formless soul soaring through time and space to distant moons and stars, while Monkman provides an absolutely mind-blowing synth solo that soars like the wind over stabs of dramatic brass. It is an absolute prog tour de force and, in my humble opinion, Curved Air's finest moment.

Finally, 'Once a Ghost, Always a Ghost' takes a more playful approach, with a melody and rhythm that jump about all over the place, accompanied by the sounds of a party in the studio. Kristina sings her own lyrics about the joys of being a ghost, while Frank Ricotti plays nimble vibes in a complicated time signature that recalls the best moments of the future Pierre Moerlen's Gong.

Phantasmagoria was hailed as the culmination of everything Curved Air had done so far, with an almost perfect blend of catchy songs, way-out instrumentals and progressive moments. But it was to lead to the first major split within the band. Kristina said (also in the liner notes):

One day, Florian, Darryl and Francis all said they were leaving Curved Air. We had all lived together since the band had begun. But I think that it had got to the stage where there was a lot of tension between some of the guys. I know that Darryl and Francis were finding it increasingly tough to work together. There was no major falling out, it was just that they both felt they had taken the band as far as they could creatively, given that the two of them had different artistic ideas.

Darryl Way told the *Mike Nelson Show* in 2022:

Francis wanted to take the band in a more experimental direction and I wanted to keep it slightly more in the commercial vein. He decided to leave and I thought I would leave as well. With the inexperience of youth, I thought I could do it all over again with another band, but of course, it doesn't work like that.

Meanwhile, Monkman blamed the band's manager, who told the band they were beating their heads against a brick wall 'and we decided to believe him'. Whatever the reasons, it was the end of a line-up that had produced three excellent albums, each one more adventurous and entertaining than the last. Curved Air would be resurrected, going on to record three more albums before splitting, followed by one last hurrah in 2008, and its ranks would boast the likes of Eddie Jobson and Police drummer Stewart Copeland.

But *Phantasmagoria* would remain the jewel in Curved Air's crown, despite being mysteriously unavailable for many years before being reissued on CD in 2007. Like the ghostly soul in the 'Phantasmagoria' suite, the music floated around in a netherworld before finally being anchored to earth once again – 'head in arm and hand in hand; we'll haunt the seven seas'.

Can - *Ege Bamyasi*

Personnel:
Holger Czukay: bass, engineering, editing
Michael Karoli: guitar
Jaki Liebezeit: drums
Irmin Schmidt: keyboards
Damo Suzuki: vocals
Recorded December 1971 to June 1972 at Inner Space Studio in Weilerswist,
Germany
Recorded by Holgar Czukay
Produced by Can
Side one: 1 'Pinch' 2 'Sing Swan Song' 3 'One More Night' Side two: 1 'Vitamin C'
2 'Soup' 3 'I'm So Green' 4 'Spoon'. All tracks written by Czukay, Karoli, Liebezeit,
Schmidt, Suzuki.
Released in November 1972 by United Artists.
Did not chart.

The story so far...

Can were formed in Cologne in 1968 by Karlheinz Stockhausen students
Schmidt, from Berlin, and Czukay, from the Free City of Danzig (then a semi-
autonomous city-state but now Gdansk, Poland), after the former was exposed
to avantgarde music and the work of Andy Warhol on a trip to New York. An
early third member was US composer and flautist David C. Johnson. Originally
focussed on classical music, band became more of a rock group with the
addition of Bavaria-born guitarist Karoli and drummer Hans' Jaki' Liebezeit
from Ostrau, near Dresden, leading Johnson to quit over new direction. The
band name was chosen because, in Turkish, it meant 'life, soul, heart, spirit,
beloved and vitality'. It could also be an acronym for Communism, Anarchism
and Nihilism. US vocalist Malcolm Mooney joined at the end of the year and the
band started recording material for an album titled *Prepared To Meet Thy Pnoom*
but could find no one willing to release it. A deliberate attempt to compose
more commercial music led to a contract with Music Factory Records, a private
label based in Munich, and the release of debut *Monster Movie* in 1969, credited
to The Can. Mooney had a nervous breakdown and was replaced by Japanese
busker Suzuki for their second album *Soundtracks* in 1970, a collection of
pieces written for films and TV. Groundbreaking double album *Tago Mago*
followed in 1971. In the same year, Can composed and recorded music for the
German-language television crime miniseries *Das Messer (The Knife)*. Theme
song 'Spoon' was released as a single and hit number six in the German charts.

The album

The young, attractive couple push through the bushes, perhaps looking for
somewhere to have a little bit of slap and tickle, or schlagen und kitzeln, as

they might say in Germany. But what they find pours cold water on their burning ardour - the body of a woman lying face down in the undergrowth, one arm outstretched, blood on her right cheek, her lifeless eyes open and blank. As the shocked couple flee across a field, the theme music follows them, rhythmic, dark, insistent, with a repetitive vocal and clanging guitar chords.

This was the opening of a three-part German crime series called *Das Messer*, translated as *The Knife*. Despite having an all-German cast speaking their language, it was actually set in Britain - it was an adaptation of a book by Francis Durbridge, creator of the Paul Temple novels and TV series, and the main character, played by Hardy Kruger, was a Scotland Yard detective.

The theme also came from an unlikely source, a chaotic, improvisational experimental rock band that combined hard, repetitive industrial rhythms with musique concrete. Can had composed and recorded music for a successful 1970 TV film *Das Millionenspiel*, so were invited to score *Das Messer*. Keyboardist Irmin Schmidt told *Uncut* magazine in 2021:

> We did our best, and then when I came with the music to the editing room, the director (Rolf von Sydow) flipped out – he didn't like the music at all. He said, 'I wanted commercial music and not some avant-garde music.' He was totally against it. Big trouble - but the guys who actually commissioned the music loved it, and said, 'No matter what the director says, this music should remain - it's fabulous.' That was a few days of sleepless nights because I thought we had done it all in vain.

In the event, the mediocre TV series was panned, but everyone praised the music as extraordinary, even though the lyrics had absolutely nothing to do with the content of the show - in fact, they had nothing to do with anything at all, although they did mention a spoon. The director was lucky - Can rarely recorded songs that were commercial enough, let alone short enough, to become hit singles. In fact, the band could be bad for your mental health, as a psychiatrist told original vocalist Malcolm Mooney, whose pained, ranting vocals make debut album *Monster Movie* such an uncomfortable listening experience.

His replacement was found busking outside a Munich cafe. Damo Suzuki improvised his lyrics on the spot, frequently singing them in an unknown language, and his words for the hit single make absolutely no sense whatsoever - 'Carrying my own in the afternoon / Hiding a spoon she will be soon / Waiting fork brings a knife / Spends me her joke, she slips me alive' he warbles in a voice uncannily like Daevid Allen from Gong. But he managed to withstand the chaos until 1973 when he left to become a Jehovah's Witness.

That's not to say everyone else in the group was totally mainstream. Drummer Liebezeit insisted on playing with a monotonous beat after a fan practically ordered him to do so in a jazz club and dedicated his life to understanding the secrets of rhythm (and once attacked Czukay with an axe, it was claimed). Schmidt had studied to become a conductor and concert pianist, and was a pupil in Stockhausen's contemporary music course in Cologne, until he realised that Sly Stone, James Brown and The Velvet Underground were also 'contemporary'. Czukay was fascinated with shortwave radio and also studied under Stockhausen before becoming a music teacher. He discovered rock music when a student played him The Beatles' single 'I Am The Walrus', which also used blasts of radio noise.

So Can seemed to drift into experimental progressive rock by accident, just as they accidentally became Germany's go-to band for quirky TV themes. When 'Spoon' became a hit, they were under pressure from United Artists to capitalise on the success with an album. 1971's *Tago Mago* had been well received, but critical acclaim had not translated into commercial success. Now the record label had Deutschmark signs in its eyes. The band's newfound popularity was further established when Can staged a free festival that drew 10,000 eager fans, playing for six hours straight at a Berlin university.

Briefly flush with funds, they set up their own studio in an abandoned cinema outside Cologne; previously Can had recorded in a castle, using the stairwell as an echo chamber. The new setup was called Inner Space and contained a self-made eight-track mixing desk, three two-track tape machines and four microphones, with old military mattresses attached to the walls to deaden the echo. Even in 1972, this was comparatively primitive equipment compared to the 24 tracks some bands were already using.

What Can would do for all their albums at this time was record - constantly. They would set the four mics up to get the best sound and then start improvising to Liebezeit's rock-steady beats, recording on one of the two-track machines. Once they thought they had something they could use, they would manually edit it by cutting and splicing the tape with a trusty razor blade, creating a backing track that would be played on one machine while they recorded live overdubs on another two-track. The third machine gave them the ability to add even more electronic bells and whistles if necessary. And that would be it, because any further copying would ruin the sound quality and increase tape hiss. Czukay explained to *terrascope.co.uk* music website:

What we did was not improvisation in the classical jazz sense, but instant composition. Like a football team. You know the goal, but you don't know at any moment where the ball is going. Permanent surprise. Editing, on the other hand, is an act of destroying. And you should not destroy something if you don't have a vision to establish it afterwards. If you have that vision, you can go ahead and do that. Can was a band. The editing had to be handled carefully, because it could destroy the character of the band.

The new studio also played its part in determining the sound of *Ege Bamyasi*. The drums were not as heavy as before, the vocals separated out - basically, Can had become just a little bit more professional and sophisticated in their recording techniques. But they still had joint responsibility because they recorded together, and that didn't change until *Landed* in 1975 when, with 24 tracks, individual members could tape their contributions on their own. For some fans and members of the band, this destroyed the collaborative and immediate nature of their work.

Recording for *Ege Bamyasi* began in December 1971, with Czukay acting as engineer, but didn't go smoothly. Schmidt and Suzuki were obsessed with chess and locked in epic battles that kept them hunched over a board instead of in front of a microphone. As the deadline approached for submitting the finished album, the band realised they were woefully short of material. The night before the deadline, they improvised the ten-minute track 'Soup', and United Artists then added the hit single. Shortly after completing the album, guitarist Karoli suffered a perforated ulcer that was nearly fatal.

The title and cover artwork came from a can of vegetables Suzuki found in a Turkish grocer's store - *Ege Bamyasi* translates as Aegean okra. This matched quite neatly with track titles such as 'I'm So Green' and 'Vitamin C', and also echoed Andy Warhol's famous 'can of soup' artwork.

The band also considered *Ege Bamyasi* to be more 'organic' than their previous work, and the album is certainly much looser and jazzier than you would expect. Despite Liebezeit's obsession with rhythm, some of the tracks actually swing thanks to his syncopated use of cymbals and snare.

Opener 'Pinch' is an obvious example - it ploughs along in the same 4/4 tempo throughout its fairly considerable 9:30 length, but Liebezeit makes full use of his kit to make things more rhythmically interesting. That's important because there is no melody here as such - Suzuki intones nonsense lyrics ('He's gonna press your ears to the light / And then I'm laughing at the way you go / Hey, that cow moaning alone') as bass and slightly funky guitar alternate between E minor and A major. There are a few electronic noises on top, but this is mostly a drum and muttering duet. Things pick up a little towards the end as the guitar comes more to the fore, ending on a sudden chord and the final word, 'Pinch'.

'Sing Swan Song' is a ballad in three-quarter time that opens with the sound of running water and features sparser drums, electronic swoops and Suzuki actually singing some kind of a melody over the chords of A minor, D and E minor. Once again, the words are pretty meaningless and seem to have been chosen for the sounds they make, while a very restrained Karoli finger-picks two or three notes in each chord.

'One More Night' hops along in a boppy 7/4 time signature, as Suzuki sings such lines as 'One more Saturday night', 'One more suck at your life' and 'One more thinking you lie', using the same six-note melody over and over again. It's all in the key of E and the only other adornment is the occasional bluesy guitar note.

'Vitamin C' comes across as a slightly slower version of 'Pinch' in exactly the same key. But there's a bit more variety here, with a funky bass drum line that sounds machine-generated, and a repetitive bass guitar riff. There's even a chorus of sorts, the first one on the album, in which Suzuki sings: 'Hey you! You're losing, you're losing, you're losing, you're losing your vitamin C.' It seems to be about a girl from a wealthy family who is 'living in and out of tune' and appears to be suffering from the titular vitamin deficiency.

It fades out on some electronic squeaking that leads into track six, 'Soup'. As mentioned above, it was recorded in one improvised take with no overdubs, the night before the finished album was due to be delivered to the record label. It opens with gentle, rhythmic percussion, wah-wahed guitar and Suzuki's indistinct voice muttering about 'the fregging town' when, suddenly, it changes tempo into something louder and funkier, Karoli supplying almost Chic-like guitar chords and the bass bopping about all over the place.

Things change again halfway through - the band speed up, stop abruptly and then there's a slow section of random noises and string scraping, with Suzuki asking, 'Is it a mind or is it a grawl?'. This disintegration of the track continues for five minutes until it ends with a crash of cymbals. Czukay said 'Soup' was his favourite track, and it became the second piece of TV music on the album, used for 'Dead Pigeon on Beethoven Street', an episode of the German crime series *Tatort*.

'I'm So Green' comes very close to being a pop song with its funky beat and guitar chords, and surprisingly tuneful singing by Suzuki. It's difficult to tell from the lyrics whether Suzuki means 'green' in the ecological sense or as a synonym for naive - it could well be the latter as it seems to be about his ability to feel everything. It fades out after, for Can, a very concise 3:06.

Finally, we come to 'Spoon', the hit single that started the album off in the first place. It's a dark but surprisingly sprightly little number, with Liebezeit playing along to the slightly Latin rhythm of a drum machine. Schmidt supplies reedy keyboard chords, Karoli little guitar riffs, Suzuki a hypnotic, repetitive melody and someone - perhaps Czukay - offering what sounds like an electronic impression of a cuica, a Latin friction drum.

The album didn't match the success of the single - the hit was surrounded by music that was simply too idiosyncratic to be appreciated by mainstream record buyers. But it has since come to be regarded as a prime slice of experimental krautrock, and a major influence on several music genres that came after. Apart from the obvious debt owed to the band by Kraftwerk and Neu!, you can also hear the Talking Heads and Public Image Ltd in its blend of mechanical rhythms and tight funk - in fact, PiL founder John Lydon applied to be Can's singer but was turned down because the band had just broken up.

Can went on to release more acclaimed albums in the 1970s, but *Ege Bamyasi* was the one that successfully married the industrial and organic sides of the band to produce something unique, influential and definitely prog.

Banco Del Mutuo Soccorso - *Banco Del Mutuo Soccorso & Darwin!*

Personnel:
Pierluigi Calderoni: drums, timpani
Vittorio Nocenzi: organ, harpsichord, synthesiser
Renato D'Angelo: bass guitar, double bass
Marcello Todaro: electric guitar, acoustic guitar, trumpet, backing vocals
Gianni Nocenzi: piano, clarinet
Francesco Di Giacomo: lead vocals
Banco Del Mutuo Soccorso recorded in 1972
Produced by Sandro Colombini
Label: Dischi Recordi
Release date: 3 May 1972
Chart places; Italy: 5
Tracks: 'In Volo', 'RIP (Requiescant in Pace)', 'Pasaggio', 'Metamorfosi', 'Il Giardino del Mago (...Passo Dopo Passo.../...Chi Ride E Chi Geme.../...Coi Capelli Scviotti Al Vento.../ Compenatrazione)', 'Traccia'
Lyrics by Francesco Di Giacomo and Vittorio Nocenzi, music by Vittorio Nocenzi
Darwin! recorded in 1972 at Ricordi Studios
Produced by Sandro Colombini
Engineered by Walter Patergnani
Label: Dioschi Ricordi
Release date: December 1972
Chart places: Italy: 4
Tracks: 'L'Evoluzione', 'La Conquista Della Posizione Eretta', 'Danza Dei Grande Rettili', 'Cento Mani E Cento Occhi', '750,000 Anni Fa...L'Amore?', 'Miserere Alla Storia', 'Ed Ora Io Domando Tempo Al Tempo Ed Egli Mi Risponde... Non Ne Ho!'
Lyrics by Francesco Di Giacomo and Vittorio Nocenzi, music by Vittorio Nocenzi

The story so far...

After studying piano, clarinet, church organ, harmony and ethnomusicology (and doing a degree in History and Psychology), Marino-born Vittorio Nocenzi performed in radio and theatre shows before writing the music for a 1968 album by actress and singer Gabriella Ferri. Through Ferri, he got an audition with RCA for a band that didn't actually exist – he had to quickly put one together with his brother Gianni, whimsically named Banco Del Mutuo Soccorso, which translates for the non-Italian speakers among us as Bank of Mutual Relief. In addition to the Nocenzi brothers, the early line-up included Gianfranco Coletta on guitar, Fabrizio Falco on bass and drummer Mario Schilli. By the time the band recorded three songs for RCA that were released on a compilation album, Claudio Falco had replaced Coletta on guitar and Franco Pontecorvi was the drummer. There were more personnel changes through 1971 as the band became known on the festival circuit, eventually settling down as the line-up listed above, including Caldoroni and Todaro from Rome and singer Di Giacomo from Siniscola. Signed to Milan record company Dischi Ricordi, Nocenzi took his band into the company's studios to record their first album.

The album

Banco Del Mutuo Soccorso were almost an Italian supergroup before they had recorded a note. Formed by the musical genius that was Vittorio Nocenzi, along with his brother, Gianna, and members of two top Italian groups, Fiori Di Campo and Experience, the band was inevitably going to make its mark in progressive rock. They are still going strong 50 years later, releasing their nineteenth studio album (if you include a couple of re-recordings), *Orlando: Le Forme dell'Amore,* in 2022.

The reason why this book places them second only to Premiata Forneria Marconi is because Banco, as they later became known, took longer to find fame outside of Italy. And, in Francesco Di Giacomo, they had a vocalist who divided opinion – his mixture of Italian operatics and Family's Roger Chapman warble was either unique and distinctive or utterly ludicrous.

They certainly had a good Italian prog name, one that was far too long and made little sense. It was inspired by the insurance companies founded by Italian peasants to help people through times of austerity and hardship – a sort of self-created social welfare system. The English word 'bank' comes from the Italian 'banco', which originally meant the bench on which Italian moneylenders would count out the cash.

When Nocenzi formed Banco Del Mutuo Soccorso (hey, let's just save paper and call them Banco – after all, that's what they did from 1978 onwards) at the tender age of just seventeen, it was as a beat group – by 1971, when he met Todaro, Di Giacomo, D'Angelo and Calderoni at the Caracalla Pop Festival in Rome, he had ambitions to merge pop with the classical music he and his brother loved.

In a 2006 YouTube interview, Nocenzi recalled:

In the 60s and the 70s, the nature of composing and performing music and its structure had completely changed ... we had abandoned the quick, three-minute verse, chorus, verse song to explore more complex territories which were richer in terms of fantasies and images. The songs could be 39 seconds or nineteen minutes long. The issue of radio airplay was not present any more ... there was an international movement of young people putting the emphasis on lyrics that were not limited to a simple love song cliche, lyrics that dealt with more profound and complex themes, often with reference to literature. The key element was more freedom to write.

With two classically trained keyboard players in brothers Vittorio and Gianni, it was inevitable that the Banco sound would be dominated by piano, organ and synthesiser, and that it would be packed full of Renaissance and Baroque influences. Rare is a Banco track that doesn't allow one or the other (or both) of the brothers an opportunity to produce something that Henry VIII could have danced to. That's not to say that guitarist Todaro doesn't get a look in, but his work is supportive rather than stand-out.

What made Banco recognisable was Di Giacomo – a big, bearded, bear of a man with a voice that oozed operatic passion, and was often described as the closest prog had to Pavarotti. It no doubt helped that Di Giacomo, along with Nocenzi, was also the lyricist for the band, so when he sang, it came from the heart.

When it comes to musical style, it is inevitable that Banco drew on many of the British 1970s prog outfits, particularly those that had some sort of classical pretensions, such as Emerson, Lake & Palmer (they were later signed up by ELP's Manticore label) and Gentle Giant. They were adept at mixing light and dark, at leaping from a wild rock workout to a wistful flute and piano instrumental, then into a doom-laden, pounding climax with washes of synth and organ and even the occasional vocal growl.

The eponymous debut album, released in May 1972, shows from the off that Banco had a sound that was already fully-fledged and confident. Opening with the unique combination of spooky, sci-fi mystery and Renaissance folk of 'In Volo (In Flight)', the band exhorts the listener to 'unleash your flight where the work of man is most ferocious/But don't deceive me with false images'. After that comes the first of three tracks that were destined to become Banco classics, 'R.I.P. (Requiescant in Pace) (R.I.P. (Rest in Peace))'. Guitar and drums lead a fast and furious track in which Di Giacomo unleashes his powerful tenor on lyrics referencing 'horses' bodies and broken spears tinged with red', before a lengthy instrumental section featuring lead guitar and piano. A sudden quiet descends in the middle as Gianni plays a mournful piano solo and Di Giacomo proclaims plaintively over the top before the rest of the band join in for a dramatic, emotional finish over speaker-rumbling church organ chords.

A brief harpsichord and vocal interlude, with footsteps walking away at the end, leads us to the eleven-minute 'Metamorfosi (Metamorphosis)'. Once again, the band explode into action with a fast guitar riff over pounding drums, before church organ chords transpose the song into a different key for hypnotic piano arpeggios. That's followed by some slithering guitar sound effects that lead into an organ solo that starts gently and tentatively before turning into a kind of musical duel between organ and guitar.

Drums take us into what could almost be a dramatic moment from a spaghetti western before another contemplative section featuring electric lead guitar over acoustic piano. The first brief vocals on the track enter at the eight-and-a-half minute mark – Di Giacomo sings something like, 'Man, I do not know if I look like you. I do not know, I feel that I don't want to mark my days with yours'. After that, repeated cries of 'No! No! No!' take us into a near-copy of the fast and furious opening and a big finish at the 10:53 mark.

The final track, and the longest at 18:27, is 'Il Giardino del Mago', which translates as 'The Magician's Garden'. It's split into four parts, opening with mysterious organ and bass notes, like the soundtrack to a prowling burglar, for the appropriately named '...passo dopo passo...' (...step by step...). Ghostly 'aahhs' float over the top, before electric guitar takes up the intricate riff. Dropping back to just a single keyboard note, Di Giacomo sings of quietly galloping his horse to the magician's garden (presumably, the horse is wearing slippers). Things speed up in part two – '...chi riode e chi geme...' (...people laugh and groan...) – when the singer arrives at the magician's garden, darting back and forth between the chords of C# minor and E minor, while the band sings 'Rule the stars! Rule the stars!'.

A sombre section with long organ chords and echoing electric guitar notes gives way to piano and occasional acoustic guitar in a minor key, with Di Giacomo singing 'How strange the sun is today, It doesn't get dark, for some reason. Maybe the evening won't come and kill me again'. Things speed up again, with both keyboard players trading lightning-fast notes off each other over a fast version of the previous piano-led melody.

A drum roll brings things to a halt for part three, '...coi capelli sciolti al vento...' (...with hair loose in the wind...), opening with a two-note motif, overlaid with finger-picked acoustic guitar, which eventually takes over with a nice Renaissance-style melody. We get the last remaining vocals, pretty much repeating the melody of part two before what sounds like a big finish.

But this is misleading – we're into part four, 'Compenetrazione' (Interpenetration), an instrumental led by guitar and bass notes sounding uncannily like Canterbury legends, Caravan, that eventually switches between the same chords as in part two, with wailing keyboard solos over the top. The entire piece finally crashes to a halt with drums and piano.

Banco's debut album revealed a band that you could pretty much describe as Italy's answer to Gentle Giant, with its ability to switch effortlessly between light and dark while incorporating Renaissance and Baroque influences. Yes, the album is dominated by the Nocenzi brothers' keyboards, but that doesn't stop Banco from rocking out with as much conviction as a British prog band. No wonder the album managed to do so well in the Italian charts, helped no doubt by the unique packaging: a cover cut in the shape of a terracotta piggy bank with a 'tongue' sporting pictures of the band that slipped out through the money slot.

For their second album of 1972, *Darwin!*, Banco created what is still regarded as one of the best progressive rock albums of all time, not just for that particularly fertile year and not just in Italy. It packs even more passion, drama, heartfelt operatic singing and stupendous musicianship into its grooves than its predecessor and has rightly been called ' the proud equal of Premiata Forneria Marconi's *Per Un Amico*... in the Italian progressive rock hall of fame' (*Allmusic*).

It is a concept album inspired by naturalist Charles Robert Darwin, who published his theory of evolution in the book *On the Origin of Species* in 1859. It's probably fair to say he didn't expect it to inspire the creation of one of 1972's most celebrated progressive rock albums. After all, he died in 1882, some 85 years before the very first prog release, *Days of Future Passed*. But he would have recognised a fellow academic in Nocenzi, a polymath who not only studied music at the Santa Cecilia Conservatory in Rome but also did degree courses in History and Psychology at the University of Rome.

Perhaps it was during a lecture on Evolutionary Psychology, which looks at how the human brain has been shaped by pressures to survive and reproduce, that Nocenzi developed an admiration for the influential English naturalist. Whatever the reason, he channelled that admiration into an album that, in musical terms, was almost as much of an eye-opener as the theories of the great man himself.

Where the debut was packed full of musical ideas and frequent shifts of style and tone, *Darwin!* is a more structured and disciplined album, and is all the better for it. There is one big beast, the opening track 'L'Evoluzione (Evolution)', that serves as an introduction to the main concept. With lyrics again by Di Giacomo and Nocenzi, the former sings (in Italian, of course) of how 'nothing was made by the Great Gods, but Creation had been created by itself: cells, fibres, energy and heat'. There are clouds of gas and spurting lava that boils the old 'primordial soup' into a life-giving broth before 'shapeless beings the sea is vomiting, pulled up in heaps on rotten shores, the earth is housing the muddy crowds. Crawling they climb on alike creatures, the time will change their flabby bodies into shapes useful to survive'. The ceiling of the Sistine Chapel it ain't.

Musically, the band provides a suitable backing for this tumultuous upheaval – mysterious, Floydian minor key organ introduces Di Giacomo over tinkling piano before we thump into dramatic, crashing chords. With the vocals rising powerfully, Todaro gives us some tasty guitar licks over the swelling keyboards.

There's a brief lull before we enter a faster, more rocking section with breathless vocals, a frantic piano solo and gritty lead guitar, all over swirling, jazzy organ. The middle of the track is dominated by wonderful keyboard interplay and Gianni's clarinet battling it out for supremacy before a slow, menacing section in which a bass keyboard note treads heavily like a giant's footsteps. Then it's back into a repeat of the rocking verses, followed by gentle baroque keyboard flourishes, culminating in a reprise of the opening vocal melody and a big instrumental finish.

Yes, it sounds disjointed when laid down on paper, but it all holds together well across a shade under fourteen minutes and demonstrates the power of the brothers' duelling keyboards.

'La Conquista Della Posizione Eretta' (The Conquest of the Standing Position) is mostly instrumental, and gives us hints of Camel in its pounding opening, and ELP in the keyboard, bass and drums interplay. The brief lyrics, which appear about six minutes in, suggest a somewhat unscientific interpretation of the change from quadrupedal to bipedal transportation, in which an unnamed creature discovers standing on his own two feet gives him a better view, so he decides to stay like that.

Side two opens with what sounds like a jazz quartet of piano, bass, drums and guitar, before the organ jumps in, playing a sprightly little minor key tune in three-quarter time. The title, 'Danza Dei Grande Rettili', translates as 'Dance of the Great Reptiles', although I doubt any brontosaurus was as light on its feet as the music suggests.

'Cento Mani E Cento Occhi (A Hundred Hands, A Hundred Eyes)' tells of Mankind's ability to work together, and how that helped human beings achieve dominance on the planet. The keyboards open proceedings with what sounds like a brass fanfare before settling into a driving rhythm in 10/4 time (perhaps), interspersed by off-kilter vocals, quiet piano passages and ending with a faster section that could be Genesis in 1971, with guttural chanting over the top.

Things slow down a bit for '750,000 Anni Fa...L'amore?', which translates as 'Love 750,000 Years ago' – a hairy male ape watches a pale female creature slipping into the shallows of a stream, and he's not appreciating her for her mind. This plays out over gentle piano figures with occasional dramatic synth interjections.

Pulsing bass notes open 'Miserere alla Storia' (Lament to History), a mostly instrumental piece that, again, shifts from slow and dark to, well, fast and dark. The sparse and obscure lyrics reference the Tower of Babel, the biblical legend that tries to explain the proliferation of languages across the planet.

The album ends with the wordy 'Ed Ora Io Domando Tempo Al Tempo Ed Egli Mi Risponde... Non Ne Ho!' (Ask Time For More Time and He Answers Me... I Don't Have Any!), a merry-go-round waltz with a chorus that sounds suspiciously like 'Home on the Range'. The subject matter is the 'eternal wheel' that grinds us all down 'crushing my bones and my will'.

Initially only released in Italy, *Darwin!* had to wait until Banco became more known during the 1980s to receive international acclaim and for the album to take its rightful place as one of the best progressive rock recordings of 1972. The band re-recorded the album in 1991 because they were never happy with the original production, but to get that authentic 70s sound, only the original will do.

Bo Hansson – *Music Inspired by The Lord of the Rings*

Personnel

Bo Hansson: organ, guitar, Moog synthesiser, bass guitar

Rune Carlsson: drums, congas

Gunnar Bergsten: saxophone

Sten Bergman: flute

Recorded late 1969 to early 1972 at Bo Hansson's summer house in Algo, Stockholm County, Sweden, and Studio Decibel, Stockholm

Produced and engineered by Anders Lind and Bo Hansson

Label: Silence Records (Sweden), Charisma (UK), Buddah (US)

Release date: Sweden in December 1970 as *Sagan om Ringen*, UK in September 1972, US in October 1972

Chart places: Australia: 31, UK: 34, US: 154

Tracks: 'Leaving Shire' (Första vandringen) 'The Old Forest & Tom Bombadil' (Den gamla skogen/Tom Bombadil), 'Fog on the Barrow-Downs' (I Skuggornas rike), 'The Black Riders & Flight to the Ford' (De svarta ryttarna/Flykten till vadstället), 'At the House of Elrond & The Ring Goes South' (I Elronds hus/Ringen vandrar söderut), 'A Journey in the Dark' (En vandring i mörker), 'Lothlórien', 'Shadowfax' (Skuggfaxe), 'The Horns of Rohan & The Battle of the Pelennor Fields' (Rohans horn/Slaget på Pelennors slätter), 'Dreams in the House of Healing' (Drömmar i Läkandets hus), 'Homeward Bound & The Scouring of the Shire' (Hemfärden/Fylke rensas), 'The Grey Havens' (De grå hamnarna) All tracks composed by Bo Hansson.

The story so far...

Born in Gothenburg, Sweden, but raised in a remote pine forest, Bo moved to Stockholm, where he learned to play guitar and performed in local beat groups. Switching to Hammond organ, he teamed up with drummer Janne Carlsson, forming a successful duo that released three albums between 1967 and 1969. The duo broke up when Carlsson went into TV, so Hansson started writing music based on JRR Tolkien's *Lord of the Rings*.

The album

'By God, not another bloody elf!' exclaimed the writer CS Lewis (or it could have been Oxford don Hugo Dyson; there are conflicting stories) when forced to listen to another instalment of his friend Tolkien's fantasy saga.

I must admit, I'm with Lewis (or Dyson) on this one. I leafed through The Hobbit once but was underwhelmed. And, after sitting through the first interminably long *Lord of the Rings* movie, I decided life was far too short to see any others.

But there was a time when Tolkien was considered prog literature (maybe it still is) and no self-respecting prog rock fan could be seen without a dog-eared copy. It certainly found its way into music, with bands such as Led Zeppelin, Rush, Camel and Megadeth recording songs inspired by the stories. Mostly Autumn and Glass Hammer have produced their own Rings-themed albums, while Marillion took their name from another Tolkien book, *The Silmarillion*.

Bo Hansson, however, was the first to produce a *Lord of the Rings* concept album, one that took a few years to break out of Sweden and make its way to other music-listening parts of the world. If you are Swedish, then this is a 1970 album, and you may be wondering how it got into this book. But if you are from Europe, the US or Australia, Bo's LP was one of the prog rock hits of 1972.

For Bo, it all started with American jazz organist Eugene McDuff, sometimes known as 'Brother' or 'Captain' Jack McDuff. One night, guitarist Bo walked into a jazz club in Stockholm and saw 'Brother' Jack playing Hammond organ, making music with both his hands and his feet (by pressing the bass pedals). Like Bo, McDuff had begun his career playing a stringed instrument – bass guitar in his case – but switched to organ in the late 1950s.

From that moment on, Bo wanted to play Hammond organ. But they were expensive instruments in those days, so he and former bandmate Bill Ohrstrom hit on a cunning plan. They would go into music shops, claiming to be interested in buying an instrument, and Bo would sit down at the Hammond organ to 'try it out'. Then Bill would pretend to be called away on another errand for a couple of hours while Bo would continue playing as if he was 'waiting for him'. Then the pair would give the manager their thanks and leave the shop.

By touring all the music shops in Stockholm, Bo put in a fair amount of practice before, eventually, buying his own instrument on an instalment plan. According to his biography on the Silence Records website, his friends vouched for him, later regretting it because Bo didn't pay the instalments and they were left picking up the bill.

In the meantime, Bo's purchase gave his music career a much-needed boost, enabling him to form a jazz fusion duo with drummer Janne Carlsson. As Hansson and Karlsson – the latter was a misprint that they kept – Bo had his first taste of commercial and artistic success. The three albums they recorded together are seen as early pointers to progressive rock. They even supported Cream in Stockholm and jammed with Jimi Hendrix, who recorded one of their songs, 'Tax Free', released on the posthumous 1972 album *War Heroes*.

When the duo broke up, Hansson retreated to a friend's apartment with a copy of Tolkein's fantasy novel *Lord of the Rings*, given to him by a then-girlfriend. Charmed and captivated by the book and its stories of dwarves, elves, hobbits and dark lords – and there's a ring involved, I do believe – Bo was inspired to compose some music on his new organ, making such a racket that he managed to get himself evicted.

He turned up on the doorstep of sound engineer Anders Lind, who was a big Hansson and Karlsson fan and had recorded the duo's live album, as well as the Hendrix jam session. Lind loved the demos Bo had produced. In an interview for this book, he said: 'He knew I had some technological equipment and also a little record company called Decibel Records. I was stunned by the uniqueness of his new music and said I'd gladly help him to record it'.

The pair borrowed a four-track Telefunken tape recorder and pooled their limited resources to buy some tapes and rent a summer house on a remote island in the Stockholm archipelago – it was winter, so it was cheap. Anders told me:

For drums, Bo invited his friend, Rune Carlsson. The original sessions were made with these two only and Bo played organ, guitar, bass and both of them some percussion. Later on in the spring, we went into Decibel 'speech studio' and transferred the tapes to an eight-track 1" tape machine for additional instruments like flutes and saxophones played by Bo's friends, Sten Bergman and Gunnar Bergsten. We also did some choirs in a church and Bo played Moog synthesisers on some songs.

The album was the first release on Anders' new Silence label. *Sagan om Ringen*, which translates literally as Saga of the Rings, was a modest success in Sweden and received a fair amount of radio play, although it failed to trouble the charts. But it enabled Bo to buy a summer house and musical instruments to continue making music. Anders said: 'The album also meant a good deal for the Swedish musical scene and inspired many groups to do instrumental albums'. In the meantime, Anders tried to interest other companies in releasing the record outside Sweden. He told me:

I met with the manager for a Swedish group called Mecki Mark Men, who were friends of mine, and they were on a tour in the States and he said he would help me to release the album there. I went over to meet them all and spend some time there, including helping them with an album in Chicago Chess studios, but for me and Bo and Silence, it turned into nothing. Yes, he is said to be a former manager of Jayne Mansfield, but what do I know?

Major international success had to wait until two years later when someone – Anders doesn't know who – sent a copy of the album to Tony Stratton-Smith, boss of Charisma Records. Charisma was the home of Genesis, Lindisfarne and the later short-lived career of The Nice – all British folk-rock or progressive acts. So Stratton-Smith was going out on a limb by licensing a foreign album for release in the UK and the US.

He immediately ran into trouble from Allen and Unwin, the British publishers of Tolkien's books, who objected to the title and to a plan to put female voices on some new material recorded by Bo that appeared on the worldwide release and subsequent Swedish pressings. That's why the 1972 release, and most subsequent releases, are titled *Music Inspired by Lord of the Rings*.

So what inspired music do we find within the grooves? Bo's work is eerie and sparse, the swelling and receding organ sound full of foreboding, his guitar providing simple but memorable melodies while the drumming is heavy on muted tomtoms and washes of cymbal. Sometimes it channels early David Gilmour – indeed, the entire album is quite Floydian with its menacing ambient soundscapes, insistent repetition and swooping guitar sounds.

There are a lot of fog and forests involved in *Lord of the Rings* and Bo's compositions certainly seem to be the perfect accompaniment to treading carefully through a claustrophobic, perhaps perilous landscape. Things pick up a bit in tracks such as 'The Black Riders', in which an undulating melody line is accompanied by frantic bongos, and 'The Horns of Rohan', in which muted sections are interspersed with sudden, rushing blasts of fuzz guitar set once again to rhythmic percussion.

Musical themes are established, fade away and then return later in a different form, while the album ends with the sound of waves on a beach – The Grey Havens which, in the book, are located on the shores of the Gulf of Lune. Some elves probably live there.

Why did Bo's album strike such a chord with progressive rock fans across the world? Anders told me: 'I think maybe it is for the melodies and his personal way of playing and that he catches the "feeling" inside the story'. *Allmusic* certainly appreciates it, calling it 'one of the few progressive rock instrumental recordings that still holds up on repeated listening' with a 'rich sonic palette'. It is an early example of an almost solo work by a multi-instrumentalist, predating Mike Oldfield by two years, and has been hailed as an early example of so-called 'space rock'.

Bo released three more instrumental albums in the 1970s, two of them produced by Anders, but none came close to matching his inspired debut. After a fifth and final album in 1985, he gave up on the music industry and became something of a recluse, dying in Stockholm in 2010 at 67.

But his music lives on as the perfect accompaniment to reading Tolkien's epic while puffing on something naughty – although, personally, I would set fire to the book.

Uriah Heep – *Demons and Wizards*

Personnel:
David Byron: lead vocals
Mick Box: guitars
Ken Hensley: keyboards, guitars, percussion, vocals
Lee Kerslake: drums, percussion
Gary Thain: bass guitar
Recorded between March and April 1972 at Lansdowne Studios, London
Engineered by Peter Gallen.
Produced by Gerry Bron.
Label: Bronze Records (UK), Mercury Records (US)
Release date: 19 May 1972
Chart places: UK: 20, US: 23, Finland: 1
Tracks: 'The Wizard' (Mark Clarke, Ken Hensley), 'Traveller in Time' (Mick Box, David Byron, Lee Kerslake), 'Easy Livin'' (Hensley), 'Poet's Justice' (Box, Hensley, Kerslake), 'Circle of Hands' (Hensley), 'Rainbow Demon' (Hensley), 'All My Life' (Box, Byron, Kerslake), 'Paradise' (Hensley), 'The Spell' (Hensley).

The story so far...

In 1967 Mick Box, from Walthamstow, East London, formed a band in Brentwood, Essex, that was soon joined by David Garrick (who later changed his surname to Byron) from nearby Epping. They formed a new band called Spice and were joined by drummer Alex Napier and bassist Paul Newton. After gigs at The Marquee in London, they were managed by record producer Gerry Bron, who signed them to Vertigo Records. While recording their first album, *...Very 'Eavy ...Very 'Umble,* in 1969, the band's name was changed to Uriah Heep, a character from Charles Dickens's book *David Copperfield*, because it was the 100th anniversary of the author's death. Their debut album (released as Uriah Heep in the US) was generally panned by critics but managed a respectable number eleven in Italy, fourteen in Finland and fifteen in Australia. Napier was briefly replaced by Elton John's drummer Nigel Olsson before Keith Baker occupied the stool for the more progressive second album, *Salisbury*, released in 1971. The drum merry-go-round continued, with Iain Clark replacing Baker in late 1970 for third album *Look at Yourself*, which topped the Finnish album chart in 1971, hit number five in Japan and entered the UK Top 40 at number 39. Slowly and steadily, the Heep were getting there – but more line-up changes were to come.

The album

'If this group make it, I'll have to commit suicide', said *Rolling Stone* critic Melissa Mills about Uriah Heep's debut album. 'From the first note, you know you don't want to hear any more'. It is not known if Ms Mills carried out her threat because Uriah Heep did indeed 'make it'. And 1972 was the year when their fourth album, *Demons and Wizards*, stormed the European charts and broke them in the States.

It had been a slow and steady climb from the wilds of Essex to global success, from being dismissed as a derivative proto-heavy rock band to grudging critical acceptance from *Rolling Stone* that 'these guys are good'. They lost several band members along the way, and had a particularly *Spinal Tap*-ish problem with drummers – not that any of them exploded, of course, but the drumming stool seemed to have a new bottom on it for practically every album. But each release showed the band edging towards its own sound, gaining confidence and improved songwriting chops, with steadily growing sales and chart success.

Their 1971 US tour was everything four young British blokes could have hoped for, with endless encores and a seemingly limitless supply of willing young ladies. Heeps of them, in fact. But the rock 'n' roll lifestyle didn't suit everyone.

Founding member Paul Newton suffered a nervous breakdown during the tour for third album *Look at Yourself*, and was replaced by Mark Clarke, who also quit after just four months for fear he, too, might be driven mad by the stresses of touring. His last contribution was to help write a song Ken Hensley had been struggling with that became the title track of the next album. In a 2021 interview with *Classic Rock* magazine, Mick Box recalls:

> I remember Ken playing 'The Wizard' on an acoustic guitar in the back of our van. It was the first time I'd heard anyone play guitar with a drop-D tuning. He couldn't find a middle eight so Mick Clarke wrote that, and the whole song sounded so good to everyone. I think we knew it was something special.

But Mark wasn't the only Clarke to leave the building. Drummer Iain parted company 'by mutual consent' after a US tour and was replaced by Lee Kerslake, who had already turned down an offer to join when Keith Baker went. This time, Kerslake said yes, and was swiftly followed by a new bass player, Gary Thain, from the Keef Hartley Band. By early 1972, what is generally agreed to be the classic Uriah Heep line-up was in place. All they needed now was a classic album. In the same interview, Box said:

> Now we finally had a real steam engine of a rhythm section. Having those two powerhouses behind us provided a wonderful foundation for the band. Lee was a fantastic drummer, and Gary would come up with these great bass lines that never got in the way of the melody of the song but always seemed to enhance it. It was an incredible knack. It was a real pleasure to work with the pair of them. Everything just clicked into place.

135

And this from Hensley:

D&W was such an exciting record to write and record. The band was totally connected and there was nothing between us and the music. This liberated my creativity and the fact that FM radio in America was pioneering the musical freedom trend made it even more inspiring. Plus, I was really enjoying my songs at that time and beginning to feel the freedom and the ability to write just about anything!

The band already had one song, 'The Wizard', and it opens the album. Inspired by a recurring dream Hensley had, it starts with acoustic guitar and the sound of a whistling kettle – the band was brewing up a pot of tea in the studio while rehearsing and discovered the kettle was in the key of C, perfectly in tune with the song. Byron takes lead vocals with just the acoustic guitar as accompaniment for the first verse before the rest of the band kick in – although Mick Clarke, who makes his only album appearance on this song, sings the high melody in the middle.

Hensley's lyrics recall his night-time inspiration: 'He was the wizard of a thousand kings, and I chanced to meet him one night wandering/He told me tales and he drank my wine, me and my magic man, kinda feelin' fine'. Okay, it's not Keats, but it rhymes and scans. Interestingly, after writing the song, Hensley didn't have the dream ever again. 'The Wizard' had been exorcised.

Hensley brought five mostly completed songs to the sessions, while Box contributed riffs and musical ideas that were then worked up in the studio. One of these resulted in the second track, 'Traveller in Time', which opens with a simple, heavy riff, wah-wah guitar under the verses, poppy, bopping bass from Thain, tremendous drumming from Kerslake and fades out on a lengthy instrumental section.

The second Hensley offering is an unashamed, basic rock track that channels Deep Purple's 'Black Night' into a galloping number that had 'hit single' written all over it. 'Easy Livin'' was written in just fifteen minutes and was inspired by a comment made by one of the band as the Heep were rushing from gig to recording studio to airport to US tour, with barely a break to draw breath. 'This is easy livin', isn't it?' someone said with heavy irony, and the phrase stuck. The song was indeed released as a single, with the non-album track 'Why?' on the B-side, and was the band's only US hit, as well as charting in several European countries.

'Poet's Justice' was initially conceived as an acoustic number, but you wouldn't have guessed from the final recording, which showcases the many-tracked vocal harmonies of Byron and Hensley's nimble keyboard work in a medium-paced rocker.

'Circle of Hands' came out of a seance in Italy with some female fans. Box said: 'It all got a bit out of hand, a bit freaky. These things start out as a bit of fun, then you start to get a bit uncomfortable, and then it's "Bloody hell,

I'm getting out of here!" That was the first and last time we tried to summon spirits of the dead. We were dabbling where we should never have dabbled'.

The song opens with rich, swirling organ chords like a church hymn before the band jump in and play a simple but effective three-chord riff. Byron sings over stately organ backing and there's a repetitive twin harmony guitar phrase that dominates the second half of the track and leads it to the fade out.

Side two opens with Hensley's 'Rainbow Demon', a slow, dark blues with a heavy organ riff that provides the second half of the album's title, while 'All My Life' channels Led Zeppelin with a slide guitar riff that Jimmy Page would have been proud of and vocals that owe not a little to Robert Plant and his falsetto screams.

Another Hensley track, 'Paradise', is an upbeat ballad led by acoustic guitar that builds to a big finish with powerful drumming and slow, crunching electric guitar notes. It segues directly into the final track, 'The Spell', the most progressive song on the album. 'The Spell' clocks in at seven and a half minutes, with an upbeat, rocking intro driven by piano and organ. But it suddenly slams the brakes on and turns into a slow ballad, again led by piano, with Box playing Gilmour-ish slide guitar over harmonic 'ahhhs'. The guitar is replaced by some passionate vocals from Byron before the song heads back into upbeat territory, pretty much reprising the intro.

Graced with a distinctive Roger Dean cover that strongly suggested the band had 'arrived', *Demons and Wizards* forced a few critics to eat their words. *Rolling Stone* magazine said: 'The first side of *Demons and Wizards* is simply odds-on the finest high energy workout of the year, tying nose and nose with the Blue Öyster Cult'. *Allmusic* says the album 'finds Uriah Heep covering all the bases with style and power' and called it their finest hour.

Their second album of 1972, *The Magician's Birthday*, was less successful. The Roger Dean cover couldn't hide the pedestrian and derivative nature of most of the songs, illustrated by the Deep Purple falsetto vocals on opener 'Sunrise'. The band blamed their management for rushing them into the studio before they were truly ready in order to capitalise on their sudden success. But the ten-and-a-half-minute title track showed the band could still create interesting, even disturbing, music performed with urgency and style.

Let us leave the last word to Mr Box. In a *Classic Rock* interview in 2021, he said:

Demons And Wizards means a lot to me. Where we were as a unit, creatively, it was the band at its height, with that line-up. Listening back to the album through the speakers at Lansdowne back in 1972, we felt like we had something special, but that was just within our inner circle. After that, you just hope that it might take on a life of its own and become successful. Which, to our immense gratitude, it did.

They Also Served ...

We live in an increasingly contrary world, so I will not be surprised if your particular 1972 prog rock favourite managed to slip through the net, and you feel the irresistible urge to express your displeasure on social media. With that in mind, I include this short and sweet mention in dispatches for those bands and LPs that you probably think I should have included but didn't.

Caravan – *Waterloo Lily*

Sandwiched between the classic 1971 release *In the Land of Grey and Pink* and 1973's pop-prog masterpiece *For Girls Who Grow Plump in the Night*, the Canterbury band's fourth album is an uncomfortable excursion into more jazzy territory thanks to the replacement of original keyboard player David Sinclair with Steve Miller.

The title track and the multi-part 'The Love in Your Eye' are bonafide classics, but 'Nothing At All/It's Coming Soon/Nothing At All (Reprise)' is a mostly improvised long jazz track that meanders aimlessly and the rest is fairly forgettable.

Nektar – *A Tab in the Ocean*

A British band formed by Englishmen living in Hamburg (eh?), Nektar were unusual in that two of their six members didn't write or perform – instead, they were in charge of the light show. Their second album, *A Tab in the Ocean*, is a good, solid prog rock effort with excellent keyboard and guitar work, particularly on the seventeen-minute title track. Their best album was 1973's *Remember the Future*, which gained them some brief popularity in the US, but they never managed to get into the top tier of prog rock bands.

The Moody Blues – *Seventh Sojourn*

The magnificent Moodies released the first progressive rock album in *Days of Future Passed*, but subsequent offerings became more and more commercial until, by *Seventh Sojourn* (actually their eighth album), they had become an enjoyable but undemanding soft rock band. It has some pretty songs on it, such as 'Isn't Life Strange' and the spirited 'I'm Just a Singer (In a Rock and Roll Band)', but this is not really prog any more.

Soft Machine – *Fifth*

Robert Wyatt had gone and the remaining members, Mike Ratledge and Hugh Hopper, were heading towards jazz fusion territory. Nothing wrong with that – there's a very thin, sometimes invisible, dividing line between jazz fusion and prog rock – but they had lost some of their individuality and quirkiness. At this stage, I preferred Matching Mole.

Manfred Mann's Earth Band – *Manfred Mann's Earth Band & Glorified Magnified*

Pop star keyboard player Mann gradually introduced more interesting elements into his music before embracing progressive rock with his Earth Band. This debut is strong and assured but is probably more blues rock than prog, while *Glorified Magnified* has its heavy moments and a title track that channels King Crimson. But the band's material was rarely as strong as its playing and it relied on other songwriters such as Bob Dylan and Bruce Springsteen to supply hits. 1973's *Messin'* and *Solar Fire* are probably better examples of Mann's brand of commercial prog.

Guru Guru – *Kanguru*

A German Krautrock band that were actually a little more melodic and adventurous than some of their contemporaries. Their 1972 release consists of four songs, all around the eleven-minute mark, combining diverse rhythms with some excellent guitar work, apocalyptic vocals, electronic noises and inventive sound effects. It is still a challenging listen, though, as it's clearly all improvised with very little in the way of recognisable chord progressions.

Kraan – *Kraan*

Another album that almost made it into the main section, relegated only because hardly anyone has heard of them. But if you like your Krautrock less industrial and repetitive, perhaps even featuring elements of Zappa-esque jazz, Arabic musical scales, bizarre time signatures, soaring sax and an eighteen-minute centrepiece that channels Family, Led Zep and free jazz, then this is for you. Kraan have an impressive discography that stretches into the 21st century with 2020's *Sandglass*.

Khan – *Space Shanty*

The only album by a short-lived Canterbury band notable for containing personnel who went on to better things, including guitarist Steve Hillage (Kevin Ayers, Gong, System 7), keyboard player Dave Stewart (Hatfield & The North, National Health), and drummer Pip Pyle (Gong, Hatfield & The North and many other things). The music is spacey, jazzy prog, played well with plenty of melodic hooks but lacking some of the humour that other Canterbury bands embraced.

Supersister – *Pudding En Gesteren*

A Dutch band clearly inspired by the Canterbury Scene, combining jazzy prog with dark humour and a vocalist who bore some audio resemblance to Caravan bassist Richard Sinclair. Their 1972 offering is not as good as their two earlier albums and is not the place to start if you want to acquaint yourself with them. Try *Present From Nancy* (1970) and *To the Highest Bidder* (1971).

139

Family – *Bandstand*

Their first few albums definitely occupied prog-rock territory, but they became less interesting and more mainstream as time went on. Despite the presence of John Wetton on bass, *Bandstand* is a great rock album (with a hit single in 'Burlesque'), but it's not a great prog rock album – it's too conventional for that.

Hawkwind – *Doremi Fasol Latido*

It's no surprise that The Sex Pistols covered Hawkwind because they were always more of an early punk than prog band. The music is pretty dumb; usually a heads-down, no-nonsense guitar, bass and drums thrash with spacey synth effects. Their third album came at the height of brief commercial success thanks to hit single 'Silver Machine' – at the time of writing, they are still a going concern, having released an album, *Somnia*, in 2021. And they sound exactly the same as they did in 1972.

Electric Light Orchestra – *The Electric Light Orchestra*

Famously, the debut album by the band better known as ELO was released in the US as *No Answer*, which was what the record company got when it asked the group what the title was. ELO were meant to be a classical and rock crossover, but the first album ended up being an uncomfortable mix of Jeff Lynne's straight-ahead rock songs with added strings ('10538 Overture') and Roy Wood's bizarre cello-driven mediaeval-sounding instrumentals ('The Battle of Marston Moor (July 2nd 1644)'). Second album *ELO 2* (1973) was more successful and, of course, they turned into one of the biggest pop groups of the 1970s.

Ash Ra Tempel – *Schwingungen*

Founded by German electronic music pioneer Klaus Schulze and guitarist Manuel Gottsching, Ash Ra Tempel's 1971 self-titled debut is considered a Krautrock classic. 1972's *Schwingungen* is less so – nothing much really happens for most of side two. Gottsching went on to release albums that showcased more of his guitar work, culminating in 1977's *Blackouts* under the shortened name of Ashra.

Roxy Music – *Roxy Music*

Is there such a genre as glam prog? If not, I lay claim to having invented it, just there. In the words of *Rolling Stone*, Roxy Music combined 'nerdy art-rock and sexy glam rock' into a unique package that seemed to shamelessly plunder all manner of musical and cultural influences with a kind of cynical glee. Produced by Peter Sinfield of King Crimson – who also helmed the hit debut single, 'Virginia Plain' – *Roxy Music* hit a very respectable number ten in the UK album charts. But it was probably too glam and sparkly for prog-rock fans at the time.

Chick Corea – *Return to Forever*

As I said above, there is a thin, almost invisible, dividing line between jazz fusion and prog rock. A band that comfortably straddled both genres was Return to Forever, which featured the talents of bassist Stanley Clarke and, later, guitarist Al Di Meola. The leader was Chick Corea, and the band's first recording, credited to Corea, is regarded as a jazz-fusion classic that drew heavily on Miles Davis's experiments on *In a Silent Way* (1969) and *Bitches Brew* (1970), adding Latin influences with Brazilian percussionists.

Moving Gelatine Plates – *The World of Genius Hans*

A band formed in France by pals Didier Thibault and Gerard Bertram but influenced by the Canterbury Scene in Kent – mostly long, quirky instrumentals dominated by electric guitar and saxophone, with humorous Zappa-esque vocals (and a cover showing a man with a pig's head). Sadly, their two 1970s albums sold even more poorly than most Canterbury music, forcing a break-up.

Pekka Pohjola – *Pihkasilma Kaarnakova*

Bassist Pohjola was a member of Wigwam, one of Finland's most popular progressive rock bands, before setting off on a solo career of mostly instrumental albums. His 1972 debut channelled Frank Zappa, jazz fusion and classical leanings into an entertaining musical blend. He released better albums than this – notably, 1974's *Harakka Bialoipokku* (released in the UK as *B The Magpie*) and 1977's *Keesojen Lehto* (in the UK as *The Mathematician's Air Display*, while in some other countries, it was known as *The Consequences of Indecisions* and, strangely, credited to Mike Oldfield).

Agitation Free – *Malesch*

Some more Krautrock for you, but the debut from Agitation Free seasons its Teutonic origins with exotic Middle Eastern musical spices, thanks to the band's travels in search of inspiration. So 'Sahara City' sounds like a journey through the desert on a swaying camel before turning into a full-throated guitar workout, while the title track layers Eastern-scale guitar over a hypnotic drone.

Aquelarre – *Aquelarre*

Argentine band's debut combines unusual song structures and juttering rhythmic changes to lift what would otherwise be a straightforward rock album into something much more interesting. Guitarist Hector Starc plays a blinder on tracks such as the nine-minute 'Aventura En El Arbol'.

Renaissance – *Prologue*

Originally formed by two members of 1960s blues-pop group The Yardbirds, the band went through a number of personnel changes before settling down into what is seen as the 'classic' line-up, with vocalist Annie Haslam and guitarist Michael Dunford. *Prologue* is their third album but was viewed by the band as its 'first' as it laid down a tentative template for what followed. Much of the album delves into hard rock but tracks such as 'Sound of the Sea' presage the later, more symphonic approach.

Alquin – *Marks*
Excellent debut album from accomplished Dutch band Alquin, full of atmospheric and jazzy prog compositions with catchy melodies showcasing the sax and flute prowess of Ronald Ottenhoff. 12-minute epic 'I Wish I Could' channels Pink Floyd's 'Echoes'. Fans seem to prefer 1973's *The Mountain Queen* but *Marks* should not be overlooked.

Where Prog Went Next

In 1972, progressive rock was achieving the rare feat of balancing musical exploration, critical acclaim and commercial success. It was not to last. As other musical genres dominated the charts, prog was increasingly seen as self-indulgent and ludicrous, not helped by some bands' vainglorious and commercially-crippling excursions into more theatrical and overblown presentations. When punk music swept all before it in 1977, the old prog bands were derided as 'dinosaurs' and expected to swiftly become extinct.

Gentle Giant steadily became less challenging and distinctive until calling it a day after their eleventh and final album, *Civilian*, in 1980. Emerson, Lake & Palmer disbanded after releasing the derided *Love Beach* in 1978 – with the band looking like bare-chested Bee Gees on the cover. Curved Air came and went but didn't make it out of the 1970s. Matching Mole lasted for one more album, although Robert Wyatt went on to enjoy a critically acclaimed and occasionally successful solo career. Neu! were short-lived, as were Can (despite several reunions), while Aphrodite's Child had broken up before their 1972 classic was even released.

As for Pink Floyd, their best years were yet to come, starting with the single most successful progressive rock album of all time, *The Dark Side of the Moon*, in 1973. Subsequent releases solidified their standing as one of the world's biggest bands before Floyd splintered following the release of the double-album epic *The Wall* in 1979 and its downbeat follow-up, *The Final Cut*, in 1983 (really a Roger Waters solo album). They were resurrected in 1985 under the leadership of guitarist David Gilmour but went into hiatus again by 2006. But the huge commercial clout of the Pink Floyd name was brought to bear one more time in 2022 when Gilmour and drummer Nick Mason joined forces for a charity single for the war-ravaged people of Ukraine.

Many prog bands were under pressure to make money as well as just spend truckloads of it, which saw some of our most treasured groups changing their musical styles to something more accessible and commercial. The most obvious and successful example were Genesis, who virtually turned their back on their prog past and became purveyors of 1980s MTV-pleasing pop pap – going from 'Supper's Ready' to 'Mama' in just a few short years.

Meanwhile, Yes lost Steve Howe but gained composer and producer Trevor Rabin, and had a hit single with the AOR-friendly 'Owner of a Lonely Heart' in 1983. Subsequently, the band lurched from one line-up collapse to another, seemingly alternating between albums that touched on past glories and terrible artistic mistakes designed to satisfy record labels and no one else. Yet, at the time of writing, Yes are still touring, albeit with only Steve Howe remaining from the *Close to the Edge* line-up.

Jethro Tull also took some artistic wrong-turns, despite releasing two of their most successful albums, *Songs From the Wood* and *Heavy Horses*, in the late 1970s during the peak of punk. They embraced electronic beats for 1984's *Under Wraps* before going back to their rock roots for the Grammy

Award-winning *Crest of a Knave* in 1987. Leader Ian Anderson disbanded the group in 2011 but has recently returned with a new line-up – without Martin Barre – and some chart success with 2022's *The Zealot Gene*.

Focus dissolved in 1978, but Thijs van Leer later joined tribute band Hocus Pocus, renamed them Focus and has been steadily releasing albums over the last few decades, culminating in *Focus 11* in 2018. Another band that seemed to defy the years was The Strawbs, who disbanded in 1980 but came back a quarter of a century later with acoustic and electric line-ups and a clutch of new albums to boot. Other artists who are somehow still touring and recording some 50 years after releasing the albums in this book include Carlos Santana, PFM and the unstoppable Uriah Heep – 25 studio albums and counting.

Prog itself went through a resurgence in the 1980s, spearheaded by bands such as Marillion, Pallas, Pendragon and IQ, and a further reawakening in the late-1990s with the help of Porcupine Tree (and their busy and influential creator, Steven Wilson), The Flower Kings, Spock's Beard, The Tangent and Big Big Train.

Today, we live in what is both the best and worst times for progressive rock. The best, because never before has it been so easy to record music and market it through social media directly to those who are most likely to be interested in it. Bands have tapped into financial resources such as crowd-funding to finance music that, otherwise, may not have seen the light of day. It is possible, in many genres of music but particularly in progressive rock, to be a one-person cottage industry, recording, marketing and distributing from a back bedroom.

It no doubt helps that many of those 1970s prog rock fans who saved up their pennies to buy the latest opus are now retired with enough ready cash to afford the latest sprawling 27-CD box set, and a monthly magazine dedicated to their interests.

But it is also the worst time for prog because, thanks again to the internet, it is almost impossible to make money out of recorded music. CDs are ripped and available for free on the internet almost as soon as they are released while streaming services pay peanuts. The only reliable revenue stream is live performances, but even they dried up during the Covid lockdown. The result is that a few artists make more money than you can imagine, while the rest can only afford a packet of crisps for lunch.

Within this challenging environment, progressive rock has not only survived but has flourished. Derided, mocked and adored in equal measure, it will exist so long as there are musicians in the world who want to break boundaries, and people, like you, dear reader, who want to listen to them.